STORIES FROM A
RADICAL CONSERVATIONIST

Running
with
Rhinos

ED WARNER

GREENLEAF
BOOK GROUP PRESS

This is a work of creative nonfiction. The events are portrayed to the best of the author's memory. While all the stories in this book are true, some names and identifying details have been changed to protect the privacy of the people involved.

Published by Greenleaf Book Group Press
Austin, Texas
www.gbgpress.com

Distributed by Greenleaf Book Group

For ordering information or special discounts for bulk purchases, please contact Greenleaf Book Group at PO Box 91869, Austin, TX 78709, 512.891.6100.

Design and composition by Greenleaf Book Group
Cover design by Greenleaf Book Group
Cover image provided by Lowveld Rhino Trust

Cataloging-in-Publication data is available.

Print ISBN: 978-1-62634-227-9

eBook ISBN: 978-1-62634-228-6

Part of the Tree Neutral® program, which offsets the number of trees consumed in the production and printing of this book by taking proactive steps, such as planting trees in direct proportion to the number of trees used: www.treeneutral.com

TreeNeutral

Printed in the United States of America on acid-free paper

15 16 17 18 19 20   10 9 8 7 6 5 4 3 2 1

First Edition

Contents

Acknowledgments

BEFORE YOU GET TO A single story, I must do what authors feel a desperate need to do and readers find boring as heck: acknowledge all those people without whom this book would never have been written. It goes without saying the wonderful, sometimes ridiculous characters you are about to meet made these stories possible.

—

I tip my hat to Raoul du Toit and Natasha Anderson, who run the Conservancy Project for the International Rhino Foundation. It's difficult to find words to express my admiration for their dedication to saving these magnificent animals. The black rhino cow and calf that beautifully run across the cover were donated by the Lowveld Rhino Trust, one of the funding agencies helping protect rhinos in southeastern Zimbabwe.

I would never have found my way to conservation in Africa if it weren't for Karl Hess, Jr., founder of The Land Center and now retired from the US Fish and Wildlife Service, and Brent Haglund, president of the Sand County Foundation. I still work with Brent and Mike Jones, my good friend and partner in Resilience Science projects.

I'd also like to thank all those scientists from academia and the non-profit world who endlessly supplied me with professional reading when in 2000 I decided to "switch" careers from geology to community-based natural resource management (CBNRM)—and working with private landowners on wildlife stewardship. Thanks to you, the first three years of my new life were not wasted on fables, falsehoods, and faith—instead, they fostered the best re-education I could have received.

Thank you, Brandy Savarese, for editing the manuscript, and thanks to the whole Greenleaf team. I expected editing to be like a root canal, but in fact you made the process of editing and publishing enjoyable.

To Jackie, my wife and life partner in adventures, thank you for saying, "Go. Just go. Get outta here and go to Africa." Without your support I would have still gone to Africa but it was a lot more fun going together.

The rhino cow and calf featured on the Table of Contents page is from a sketch Jackie drew on the envelope of one of my birthday cards. This book is dedicated to you, darlin'.

Introduction

AS THE SUN SANK IN the west, the sky turned the color of faded jeans. We had paused for lunch on the banks of Zimbabwe's Chiredzi River when the shortwave radio squawked to life. Up in the Husky, a little two-seat, single-engine airplane, Raoul was receiving an update on the location of the badly injured baby black rhino the scouts had been looking for all afternoon. Members of our crew—they had been napping under a tree—rushed to gather their gear and climb into their respective helicopters, a Eurocopter owned by Paul Tudor Jones and a Robinson 44 owned and flown by John McTaggart. Blake ("Blake" was an owner of the now-defunct Chiredzi River Conservancy. No one at Rhino Ops could remember his real name!) fired up his Land Cruiser as the helicopter rotors whined into action, and we all took off in a cloud of dust. Accompanying me in the Cruiser's open back were two game scouts, Blake's ten-year-old son Peter, and the developmentally disabled, thirteen-year-old daughter of a visiting Canadian veterinarian. We hung on to the roll bar for dear life.

Blake careened down a rough dirt track, then bounced through a newly plowed maize field. I can remember thinking, *Keep your jaw shut or you'll chip your teeth*, and tossing away the fried chicken leg that would have otherwise constituted the day's lunch. At the end of the field, we picked up a game trail leading into the woods. As we headed down and around a blind turn, we were halted by a tree almost certainly pushed down by an ill-mannered elephant. Without wasting a second, the game scouts attacked the roadblock with their razor-sharp, two-foot long, machete-like pangas.

Within two minutes and a spray of wood chips flying in all directions, the track was cleared and we lurched onward into a sand wash that nearly caused us to flip over. I had taken the moment we started up to wipe my greasy and sweaty palms on my bush shorts, already filthy with rhino blood and dust, but I managed to grab hold of the roll bar again before I pitched head-over-cab into the creek bed.

Ten minutes later we found ourselves up against an impenetrable wall of acacia thorn bush. There was no way to get the Land Cruiser any closer to the field site.

So we jumped out and ran—using the helicopter noise to vector into the location of the injured baby rhino.

—

"Running with Rhinos" is not a euphemism—not when you're the ground support for World Wildlife Fund's Rhino Conservancy Project, specializing in the preservation of black rhinos.

There are two species of rhinoceroses in Africa. The white rhino, or square-lipped rhino, is a social, grazing animal. There are approximately twenty thousand, many on private game ranches in the Republic of South Africa. The white rhino is the second largest land mammal, with bulls reaching upward of 6,000 pounds. While they are dangerous to approach, they are docile compared to their cousins, the black rhinos.

The black rhino's prehensile hooked lip enables it to eat leaves and twigs of bushy plants, rather than graze. It prefers the semiarid habitat of the thorn-bush Lowveld, the savanna land of forest, grassland, and thorn-bush scrub. While it is smaller in stature than the white rhino, weighing in at a mere 3,000 pounds, it is far more dangerous. The black rhino is solitary unless with a calf. Fewer than five thousand black rhinos remain in the wilds of sub-Saharan Africa, with the largest populations in South Africa, Namibia, and Zimbabwe. About five hundred, or more than 10 percent, live on private lands in Zimbabwe.

So, another book about rhinos? Hasn't enough been written by professional wildlife biologists and amateur environmentalists?

Well, yes and yes. But they're not stories written by a long-term, non-professional volunteer—himself a scientist—who has worked for more than a decade with the veterinarians and biologists who care for rhinos in Africa. Few if any laymen like me have been invited to do what amounts to some of the most dangerous volunteer fieldwork around.

—

When I retired from oil and gas on December 28, 2000, I was the father of coalbed methane ($200 billion of wealth creation by industry) and the mother of the Jonah and Pinedale fields in western Wyoming (about fifty trillion cubic feet of gas)—a place where *everyone* in the business just knew there was no commercial gas. My partners and I, making up the smallest companies in the industry, had discovered about one-quarter of a trillion dollars of natural gas, or 20 percent of US reserves.

I began my career nearly thirty years earlier as an oil and gas exploration geologist for a major oil company. My first job after grad school was in Denver, Colorado, but I was soon relocated to New Orleans, Louisiana. That move gave me the first of what have become "Ed's Laws": Never Live East of Aurora, Colorado, or, more generally, don't work where you don't want to live!

So, I headed back to Colorado. The only job I could find was for another of the "Seven Sisters," the companies formed in the wake of the antitrust breakup of Standard Oil of New Jersey. That I was a square peg in a company of round holes wasn't the worst of it. They didn't understand my sense of humor! Needless to say, I was a total failure. When the division geologist indicated that I might start looking for another job, I had the good sense to propose a little research project for the company. I was already thinking outside the proverbial box and wanted to investigate coalbed methane—that is, producing natural gas out of coal seams. My report gave the company a ten-year head start on what at the time seemed to be a ridiculous idea, but was really the future of the industry— unconventional gas reservoirs. When I left them two years later, they threatened me with a lawsuit but settled for a "Confidentiality Agreement." They made a billion dollars off my idea and I went on to build a career on my own terms, including the discovery of the giant southwest Wyoming gas fields, Jonah and Pinedale.

In 1998, two years before my partners sold out to a major gas company, I predicted the future. "Honey," I said to my wife Jackie, "our life is about to change. After six years of never knowing if this Jonah Field thing would turn out okay, or if we were gonna go broke, we've rounded the corner. Several things are about to happen: we're gonna be rich. My partners will sell out within a couple of years—as soon as a company comes along and offers them a billion dollars—and I'll never have to work again."

I let it sink in, and then I continued. "I thought I would be the chief scientist on this project for the next thirty years. It's not going to happen that way. When they sell out to a big ol' gas company, that company is not gonna want a loose cannon like me publishing all the secrets of this geology. I'm gonna be faced with either selling out or riding a tidal wave controlled by 'big oil.' What am I gonna do?"

Jackie, an artist, knew immediately what I should do: "You should teach. You love to work with kids. You already volunteer at the Natural History museum. Just do more. You love nature and you're a natural story teller. Follow your passion."

I decided to do even more than that. I'd live the life, not just preach or teach. During all those years managing the geology on drilling rigs, I alleviated boredom by hiking around the countryside. That's right: if you had picked up my day pack when I was supervising a drilling project you would have found a wildflower book, a bird book and, I'm not making this up, a tree book. So, I really like trees. What of it? I was an oilman environmentalist. A what? Yep, an oilman environmentalist. Geologists, wherever they take up employment, are environmentalists in their hearts. This may come as a shock to you California Bambi Environmentalists. We are not the enemy. Can you imagine a young person in love with nature setting out on a career to destroy it? I don't think so. I had a career testing my scientific theories. Only the money came from private investors, not the National Science Foundation.

In my spare time while working in Wyoming, Colorado, Montana, and Utah, I'd stop at ranches and ask permission to explore their property. In the seventies, instead of "Sure, just leave the gates like you found them," the first thing out of a rancher's mouth was "You don't work for the gummint, do you?" I quickly realized I was experiencing the unintended and negative consequences of the Endangered Species Act.

"No, I work for myself. I'm an independent geologist."

"Oh, okay. How 'bout you come by for coffee tomorrow. You can tell us if we have any oil or gas potential on our spread."

Coffee, by the way, is served at 5:30 a.m. in the summer months. I made it as often as I could. I love ranchers. I love the prairie. I realized that it was the ranchers living on some of the most remote territory in the country, not some government bureaucracy in Washington, DC, who were managing critical wildlife habitat. If I were ever to change careers, part of that change would be in support of private lands conservation. If I were to work on environmental issues, it wouldn't be from the tired old John Muir-inspired paradigm that "humans are the enemy of wilderness." That had not been my personal experience at all. My good friend, Colorado State University professor Dr. Rick Knight, expressed it perfectly. He said, "The new environmentalism will work from the 'Radical Center.'

We will work with private landowners. We will foster public-private partnerships. We will promote Aldo Leopold's 'Land Ethic,' which sums up our philosophy: 'When land does well for its owner, and the owner does well by his land; when both end up better by reason of their partnership, we have conservation. When one or the other grows poorer, we do not.'" Rick is a Leopold scholar and a wildlife biologist who understands that humans are part of the conservation equation. Once in a while he lets me, an honorary professor without the corresponding academic degrees, give a lecture to his senior seminar.

—

In April 2000, Jan Prince and Dave Schumacher took me out to dinner with Karl Hess, Jr. Karl, a wildlife biologist with a PhD from Colorado State University, was interested in pursuing new projects with private landowners in the United States and indigenous peoples in Africa, specifically under the auspices of a nonprofit called The Land Center (TLC). Cute, huh?

At the end of dinner Karl said to me, "I'm going to Harare, Zimbabwe, next week to meet with World Wildlife Fund (WWF). Want to come along?"

How could I say no? At the junction of all of my paths was the opportunity to follow my emerging philosophy of radical conservationism in Africa. WWF's Southern African Regional Programme Office (SARPO) is a center for experimentation, working with local communities and private landowners. Here was my chance to export the lessons about land and wildlife management learned in Africa back home to the United States.

The only thing I enjoy more than the adventure itself is telling the stories. In *Running with Rhinos: Stories from a Radical Conservationist* I'll take you along as I cut my teeth as the ground support for World Wildlife Fund's Rhino Conservancy Project, or Rhino Ops.

I give you these experiences as they happened to me. This work is gritty. It is sweaty, sometimes scary, mostly exhilarating. It happens to human beings (it also happens to the rhinos!) who are hardworking and sometimes hard partying. They are always extremely dedicated. It may seem that I'm making fun of them sometimes, and myself as well. So, I'll let you in on a secret in advance: these crazy, dedicated maniacs are my heroes.

CHAPTER 1

Into Africa

A WEEK AFTER MEETING KARL Hess, he and I stepped off the plane after twenty-one hours in the air and passed through immigration and customs at Harare International Airport, Zimbabwe. The next morning we attended a meeting at SARPO headquarters facilitated by a tall, rangy, big-nosed fellow who placed little post-it-like notes with words or short phrases on them on a whiteboard. Mike Jones, the big-nosed fellow, was a sight more interesting than the meeting he was running.

Mike, now a consultant, had been a National Parks ranger during the Rhodesian Bush War (1964–1979), in which Black Nationalist rebel groups fought to overturn the minority white government. On February 13, 1975, Mike stepped on an antipersonnel mine—likely buried by the nationalist army—at a campsite in Mana Pools National Park. He instantly earned membership in the "One Legged Corps" of amputees. Really—I'm not making it up—there is such a club. Mike lost his right leg, almost lost his right arm, and suffered damage to his back, as well. After knowing him for a couple of years, Jackie nicknamed him "Africa's John Wayne." Mike Jones is one tough bugger and we hit it off immediately.

—

Jackie and I visited Mana Pools on our first trip to Africa as tourists in 1999. We stayed at a fly camp on the banks of the Zambezi. Our first evening, we were entranced by the prospect of dinner around a huge hewn-log table, which was pieced together and fitted around an enormous African teak tree. The table was illuminated by a wrought iron candelabra hung from a branch of the tree.

Mana Pools is possibly the most beautiful of Zimbabwe's national parks and home to an incredible diversity of birds and mammals. The western boundary is the lower Zambezi River, so the park stretches across riparian habitat into wetlands, savanna, and mopane forest.

Prior to heading out on a walking safari our first morning, the camp director warned us of a potential problem: "Last week, an elephant stomped a villager to death. The old lady tried to chase the elephant out of her maize field and it killed her. National Parks rangers then found an elephant and shot it with a Holland & Holland .375 magnum rifle. It may not have been the offending elephant but that's the typical park policy when it comes to 'problem' elephants. The last few days, we've noticed that the elephants have been especially aggressive around people."

Well, that'll get you excited for your safari!

Sure enough, about an hour into our walk, we encountered three tuskless elephants: a cow, her calf, and an auntie walking single file. There were seven of us: our guide in front, a National Parks ranger with his trusty H & H rifle, four guests including me and Jackie, and the guy loaded with tea and cakes bringing up the rear.

I had read somewhere that tuskless elephants, tuskless due to an evolutionary response to poaching, are more dangerous than normal. Elephants use their tusks to dig up food and to defend themselves, so without tusks, they tend to exhibit extra aggression. A tuskless mother who has been "informed" of a death in her family could be expected to be exceedingly on edge.

As I focused in on the cow with my binoculars, I felt a singular shock:

Her trunk looked as if it had been caught in a snare and severely injured. Think about the most sensitive part of your body, tighten a wire snare around it, and you get the idea. Just as I began to wonder what to do if the elephant charged, she slowed to a halt. She reached down and plucked up a wad of yellow grass, waved it in front of her to dust it off, and put it up to her mouth. Imagine my astonishment as I then saw her throw it to the ground in what looked like a fit of anger.

Her head was turned to look over her shoulder at our group and I could clearly see her eyeball looking our way. She reached down again and repeated the behavior. I was just starting to think *uh, oh*, when she spun around and flat-out charged our group. I was about to turn tail and run, expecting to hear the gunshot any second, when what I heard sounded like loud claps. *Whack! Whack!* Instead of aiming the rifle at the cow, the guide and the ranger were "applauding" her! She slid to a halt, raised her trunk into the air, trumpeted a tremendous scream, flapped her ears a couple of times, and nonchalantly walked off. What an introduction to elephant behavior!

We canoed the Zambezi on our second day. Trust me, it's not an amateur paddle. I'll remember not to brag about my canoeing expertise the next time I canoe a wild African river. Between the hippos and the crocodiles, being alert is more a mandate than it is a suggestion. Every pair had a guide in their canoe except Jackie and me. We had years of wilderness and white-water canoeing experience. But, unlike canoeing a river in North America, you have to work along the shallows of the Zambezi. If, God forbid, you have to cross a deep pool, be prepared to paddle like a maniac. Just in case, you see, there are hippos resting on the river bottom.

We could approach the animals drinking along the riverbank, from baboons to elephants, very safely via canoe. They didn't seem to mind us like they would if we were on foot. Even the enormous Nile crocodiles sleeping on the sandbars, some longer than sixteen feet, could be approached with relative safety. But not the hippos: Approach anything except hippos, we were advised. Hippos will charge boats and smash them to bits. If that doesn't spoil your day, being torn apart by those enormous hippo incisors will, let me tell you. We safely avoided any hippo run-ins, and it was a magical day.

On our third morning, the camp manager met us at breakfast. "Ed and Jackie, would it be okay if David led you on a walk? It will be his first and you will have the support of a licensed guide." David was a young college student from England working the summer as a safari company intern. We happily agreed.

David may have been a "novice guide," but he was a terrific birder and a charming young man. We had a lovely walk and, with the help of the regular safari guide, James, we must have identified at least fifty species of birds. We left by charter airplane the next day for the Luangwa Valley in northern Zambia where we concluded our first African safari.

Two weeks later, back home in Denver, I opened the *Denver Post*, our local newspaper. There was a small column in the "International News" section, just about an inch long with the headline, "British Student Killed by Lion." The unnamed student was killed in the middle of the night in Matusadona National Park. My heart sank to my boots. I can't say why, but I knew instinctively that it was David. Had he told us he was going to Matusadona on his days off? I couldn't be sure. What I was sure of in that moment is that it was David who had been killed. I was so sure that I cut the article out of the paper to prevent Jackie from seeing it.

Around 11 a.m. that morning the landline rang. It was Karen Cockburn of the Africa Travel Centre in Boulder.

"Ed, do you remember a young British student named David who was working at Mana Pools?" she asked.

Oh, shit, I thought.

Karen continued, "He was killed a few days ago while camping in Matusadona. If you have any photographs of him, his parents would be very grateful."

I got their address in England, wrote a letter describing our experience with their son, and sent them copies of the photos.

Several years later, while staying in Clive Stockil's safari lodge on the Save (pronounced Sa-Vey) Valley Conservancy, I met Clive's camp manager, who was also the wife of a professional hunter. At dinner, Clive mentioned the woman's husband, Brad.

"Do you know," he asked, "about the incident that lost Brad his safari license? He was guiding a group of young people in Matusadona in 1999. That year the lions were starving due to the high water flooding Lake Kariba that drove off the game. A pride of lions got into camp one night and dragged a British student out of his tent, killed him, and ate him."

The police report found a lioness's incisor on the cot in David's tent. She must have grabbed him and dragged him out of bed and then the rest of the pride descended on him just like they would any other prey animal.

"Clive," I replied, "Jackie and I spent three days with David a couple of weeks before that incident."

Clive looked at me with amazement. "It was a no-win situation. Brad had a choice of rounding up the rest of the clients to get them inside the vehicles, or start shooting lions."

David was already dead, having been torn apart immediately, so Brad chose not to kill the lions.

"Frankly," Clive offered, "Brad did the right thing. No matter what happened next, the government would take away his safari guide license. So today he's a professional hunter."

On the drive back to Harare a week later, Brad sat next to me in the rear of the Toyota. For five hours I wanted to ask him his side of that story. I didn't have the stones to bring it up.

CHAPTER 2

WWF and the Rhino Conservancy Project

THE MEETING AT WWF WAS boring as hell. After an hour I found myself whispering jokes to the Zimbo biologist sitting next to me. He was either very good at stifling his laughter or my comedy act was not working. Eventually we were saved by the bell: teatime. Thank God for the British Empire.

We were escorted to the garden, where every member of the WWF staff was gathered, tiny teacups balanced delicately in their big hands. I wandered around meeting and greeting. In front of a fountain, along one corner of the property, I overheard a conversation about "Rhino Ops." I walked right over and introduced myself!

—

When Jackie and I had been in Zimbabwe in 1999, I met Russell Gammon, a safari guide, and convinced him to take me with him as he tracked black rhinos on foot. Russell, an enormous, redheaded Zimbabwean of Scottish descent, took two entire days to decide that I could be trusted not to get us killed; more importantly, I had to prove to him that I could climb a tree. Believe it or not, that's a serious requirement of tracking rhinos. The last thing a safari guide wants is to be forced to shoot an endangered rhino because of the stupidity of a *mzungu* (Swahili for stupid white man, or so I've been told by a Maasai friend).

Black rhinos are crazy dangerous. You can never tell what they will do next. If there's a possibility of a charge you must be able to get out of the way. Outrunning them is not an option. Rhinos run faster. The only safe course is to climb a tree.

My opportunity finally arose at breakfast on our third morning at the camp. The three other guests, a professor from Chicago and her two female students, decided to spend the morning in camp before departing in the afternoon.

As I was thinking to myself, *Thank you, God*, Jackie, who has better intuition than anyone else I know, said, "I think I'll stay behind as well. I'd like to paint. Russell, why don't you and Ed go off?"

I turned to Russell. "Please take me tracking rhinos, Russell. Whatever happens, I don't want you to shoot a rhino. I'll take my chances." I think that finally wore him down.

We were driven over to the Tashinga Peninsula in Lake Kariba, on the northeast end of Matusadona National Park, by motorboat. I had my Minolta binoculars and my point-and-shoot camera; Russell carried his 500 Nitro Express big-bore hunting cartridges, his rifle, a backpack, and Zeiss binoculars. We each carried our tools with ease.

Within minutes of being ashore we found the spoor of a black rhino. Russell tested the wind with a little spray bottle filled with talcum powder. My adrenaline rushed. We crept forward slowly.

The countryside where we were tracking was mostly mopane forest with an understory of various acacia varieties. Mopane means butterfly in the Bantu language of the Shona people. The leaves, resembling butterfly wings, open in the early morning and close when the sun gets too hot, regulating their water loss in the semiarid environment. Incredibly, mopane also respond to overgrazing by animals, like elephants, by pumping tannic acid into their branches and leaves, making them less palatable. Mopanes are not bad trees to be around, but you've got to watch out for the acacia called the "wait a bit" or "buffalo thorn," hiding in its understory. If the wait a bit thorns hook you, you must carefully pull them apart and away from you or they will slice through your skin as easily as a filleting knife.

After walking for about fifteen minutes we stopped. Russell pulled out what can only be described in my vocabulary as a bowie knife. He proceeded to cut a half-dozen mopane branches and stick them into my belt.

"Little bit of camouflage can't but help," he said, as he filled in the space to the left and right of my prized Philmont Scout Ranch belt buckle.

We crept forward. I was certain I could hear a rhino chewing. Black rhinos are browsers. Their molars shear instead of grind and I'd become familiar with the sound of their chewing while walking with baby rhinos at the Tashinga nursery two days earlier.

We peeked around the corner of a huge African teak tree. There, not more than twenty-five meters away, was the largest bull elephant I will surely ever see in my life. This *tembo* (Swahili for elephant) had enormous tusks that curved downward and toward each other, reminding me of the wooly mammoth painting I had seen in the Denver Museum of Nature and Science. I was transfixed. After not more than a minute, the bull flapped his ears, trumpeted, and walked off.

"Eighty pounders or better," Russell whispered, marveling at the elephant's enormous tusks.

Hmm, I thought. *I swear I heard a rhino chewing. My imagination must be too active. Better focus on what is real!*

We crossed the airstrip and walked into the rhino nursery camp. Airstrips in the bush are simply flat strips of land, cleared of trees. Game really love them, so when preparing to land, the pilot must first buzz the airstrip to make sure no animals are grazing, then circle back around to land. The Tashinga airstrip that we crossed is the only access to the Kariba

Lodge. Joseph, the head warden, greeted us. After exchanging brief pleasantries in English, Joseph and Russell switched to Shona. Joseph seemed agitated. Russell signaled to me and we walked off.

"What's going on?" I inquired.

"A big bull got in among the babies as they were feeding this morning. The game scouts have spent all morning up in the trees."

"The warden didn't want to tell you where they are, right?"

"I winkled it out of him. We're headed in that direction. All I ask of you, Ed, is that you follow my directions without question."

I gotta tell you, nothing could have stirred up my blood faster than Russell's matter-of-fact instructions.

We walked at a moderate pace in a straight line, as if Russell really knew where we'd find the big black bull.

After about half a mile, we slowed way down. All of a sudden, a huge head crowned by a magnificent horn rose up over an acacia bush and turned our way. I had him sighted in my binoculars—he was maybe seventy-five meters ahead of us. Behind him, I could see movement: the calves!

I started to consider that tree. The rhino had heard us and appeared to be upset. His ears, turning independently like radar units, were so clear in my binoculars that I could see their black fringes of hair. He couldn't see us or smell us—we had the wind—but he clearly sensed something was amiss and was skittish.

All of a sudden he charged! The bull was there one second and gone the next in a cloud of dust, charging at a right angle to our position. I must have held my breath for more than a minute. Just as I let it out, he trotted back to the acacia and turned toward us again. His ears began casting this way and that, trying to locate the interlopers he knew were somewhere nearby. With a big old snort, he charged again! Only this time he charged away from us. I let out another breath and he trotted back for another go.

Russell demanded, "Ed, back out of here right now!"

I don't know how I did it, but I'm pretty sure I sprinted in reverse. Somehow I managed not to trip over anything and fall on my keister. Whatever else I was going to do at that moment, turning my back on that rhino was not an option.

—

After tracking rhinos with Russell in Zimbabwe, I was hooked. So, the talk of Rhino Ops at that WWF morning tea reeled me in. I had to know what they were up to.

The fellow I introduced myself to was slightly taller than me—meaning he's a little bit taller than short—with black hair and beard, and didn't make a very good first impression. You certainly wouldn't call him a clotheshorse unless your idea of high fashion leaned toward khaki flight overalls. Raoul du Toit was then the program manager of World Wildlife Foundation's Rhino Conservancy Project when I met him. He is now the Africa program director of the International Rhino Foundation (IRF). After eavesdropping on his conversation for a couple of minutes, I made a complete ass of myself: I promptly begged to work with them.

"Could I volunteer please, please, please?" I'm not a good beggar. I didn't much like how it felt, but I was determined to join Rhino Ops.

Raoul's reply was succinct: "No."

CHAPTER 3

Sand County Foundation

BACK IN THE STATES, I continued to work with Karl Hess, Jr., on domestic projects for another couple of months. Unfortunately, the stress of trying to create a nonprofit organization took a mighty toll on him.

I had agreed to fund a GIS survey in Africa through The Land Center. Tom Wolf, Karl's sidekick, promised to wire my money directly to the project. Instead, he paid himself his own back pay and expenses. My relationship with Karl was a casualty of the misdealings, but only temporarily. I never blamed Karl and I'm really glad I didn't. We've had a lasting friendship for more than thirteen years, during which time we have worked together on some revolutionary conservation initiatives. The other guy? Fugettaboutit!

Sometime in October 2000, I got a phone call from Brent Haglund—president of the Sand County Foundation (SCF). The Sand County Foundation, founded by Aldo Leopold's godson, Reed Coleman, is dedicated to promoting Leopold's philosophy of the land. Brent asked me whether I thought the projects developed by Karl and TLC had merit. I responded that I thought they did, but the Africa projects would have to be managed from Africa by a guy I had in mind, Mike Jones. Unbeknownst to me, Brent and Mike had known each other for years.

Brent asked me if I'd like to continue my involvement with the projects if SCF picked them up. Having been burned in my first little attempt at philanthropy, I was "once, bitten, twice shy," as they say.

"Does Sand County have audited tax returns?" I asked.

Brent, bless his soul, acted puzzled.

"Sure, Ed, we have audited returns. But wouldn't you rather see the independent audits of our projects?"

Talk about naïve. I had never heard of such a thing! I didn't know that well-managed organizations sought independent review of their work. I was amazed and encouraged.

Within weeks, I had read through SCF's past independent reviews—by famous academic and NGO (nongovernmental organization) scientists. Here was a science-based conservation organization working with private landowners and indigenous peoples supporting land stewardship using market-based economics.

Conservation on private lands, lands such as American ranchland, has always been of real interest to me. But Africa was something more, something bigger. I had been bitten by the Africa bug. Collaborating with Sand County was my means of getting back to Africa to do meaningful work.

I used to explain to people, not quite tongue in cheek, that since humans evolved in Africa, we have an "Africa" gene that can be switched on or off. Born in Brooklyn, my Africa gene had been switched off at birth. It was switched back on in May 1999, when I stepped off a plane in Maun, Botswana, and smelled the Kalahari Desert.

I wish I could convey the intensity of my first experience traveling from safari camp to safari camp across the Okavango Delta to Mana Pools, to the banks of the Zambezi River and on to the Luangwa Valley in Zambia. It wasn't the sight of Africa that transformed me; it was the smell.

Somewhere, long ago, an author said something about smell touching our emotions more strongly than any other sense. The smell of the African bush pulls at my heartstrings. Walking on the savanna touches a primal connection to one million years of evolution. For me, it is a coming home.

I've always been a cold weather kind of guy. I can stand in the wind on the top of a fourteen-thousand-foot mountain wearing shorts and a bush shirt and not get cold. Even so, it was the smell of the hot, dry, dusty thorn veld that really moved me.

Remember from your childhood the smell of brown, dried leaves underfoot in autumn? Or maybe you're more familiar with the scent of sagebrush on the Wyoming prairie. Whatever the smell, I'm sure it has remained with you. For me, now, it's the Botswana sage of the African bush. It is intensely pungent—different from western sagebrush—but it is so familiar.

There are also the remarkable African plants whose odors border on the ridiculous. The first time Jackie and I walked past a pink flowering "roast potato" bush we grinned like idiots. The damn thing really smells like baked potatoes. How pleasant compared to the "old socks" bush? Think of the nastiest, dirtiest, unwashed athletic socks you have ever smelled in your life. This little plant smells worse!

Rhinos smell good. They smell gray. They smell of dried mud and a sweetish sweat. No must, no stink. I wanted to rest my head on the flanks of a rhino and smell it.

Sand County's Africa Director

It didn't take me long to fully engage with Sand County Foundation in the United States and in Africa. I became the liaison between SCF and Mike Jones in Harare and, within a year, I became an SCF director. Mike and I saw each other four times a year. Mike would come to the United States twice a year and I would fly to Africa twice a year. We worked in Zimbabwe, Zambia, Tanzania, Namibia, and Mozambique.

On the next flight from Miami to Johannesburg, a mere fourteen hours, I had plenty of time to think. I was still flying coach then, that is, cattle car, even though I was investing great sums of money in conservation. I know it is ridiculous, but I grew up middle class and often find it ever so hard to break with a lifetime of experience. I had a long and uncomfortable time to think about what I wanted to accomplish and how. I especially wanted to work with Rhino Ops.

Therefore, if I wanted to connect with the Rhino Ops guys, I would need a plan. Really, that's what Zimbos do: They "make a plan." In fact, making a plan is such an integral part of their culture that it's usually the first response to any question involving action. "Let's make a plan" seems to be a favorite expression!

I had it! I would throw parties for all my new friends. I had already met a bunch of expats, US Agency for International Development (USAID), International Union for Conservation of Nature (IUCN), WWF staff, business people, and artists. Why not invite them all to parties with the folks at Rhino Ops. You see, the way to a scientist's heart is through cold beer! I'd entertain them and they'd let me run with the rhinos. Heck, I'd buy "bombers" of beer by the case. It was the edge I needed with them (and, coincidently it worked!).

—

Mike picked me up at the airport in his horrible old pickup truck.

"Ed," he said quietly, "I've moved to a new place and I'm going to drive you there. Mary Ann, the owner, will take care of you tonight. I have something I have to do."

I was surprised. Mike had been living in a guesthouse on the estate of a retired Chevron executive. The guy had spent his career working in the Sudan, a really dangerous place, and he and his wife had decided to retire to beautiful and safe Harare.

"What's with the new place, Mike?"

"My landlord, Tony, was murdered last night by a burglar. He heard a noise downstairs and was on the staircase when the munt shot him. I've been helping his wife pack. She's heading to London tomorrow morning."

"Jesus, Mike. Let me know if there's anything I can do," I offered.

Mike dropped me off with Mary Ann, an Irish woman, by birth, who showed me to my room.

"Mike's told me all about you, Ed. You're now part of my family. You will not pay whilst you stay with me. I can't express how much it means to me that you're here helping my country."

I started to open my mouth and utter one of my patented and pithy one-liners when I thought better of it. I have Irish friends—female Irish friends. The first rule of dealing with an Irish woman is *don't cross her.*

Meekly, I said, "Thank you, Mary Ann."

She and I immediately started planning my first party.

Mike introduced me to Meg and David Cummings during that trip. David had just retired from WWF and Meg was studying spiders in her backyard. She would become famous for her spider discoveries, identifying many new species and publishing peer reviewed papers. David was part of the Resilience Alliance, a group of scientists studying the resilience of large systems (like ecosystems) using theories developed by economics. While having tea in their yard the subject of malaria came up.

"Ed, you don't take prophylaxis, do you?" asked David.

"Not since my first trip. I try to come in winter when the mosquitoes aren't flying at night."

Meg got up and went in the house. She returned with a box of meds and handed it to me. "This is Artemether, a new Chinese herbal medicine. If you take it as soon as you feel ill, it will cure the malaria."

A Note About Malaria

For those of you who are thinking about going to Africa, the medical practice recommended by American doctors does not jive with the practice of those living daily with the threat of malaria. Years ago, the standard prophylaxis—that is, prevention—was Lariam. The US Army used the drug and discovered that it caused psychotic dreams and caused full-blown psychosis in soldiers. Naturally they kept that side effect secret for years. Finally word spread and Lariam was scrubbed as the drug of choice.

The docs then recommended tetracycline, which causes reactions to sunlight like mega-sunburn. Visiting Africa means exposure to a lot of sunshine, so tetracycline (which isn't all that effective anyway and causes your bones to fluoresce under a black light!) isn't a great choice. Big pharma finally came up with Malarone, which works well but costs a fortune. What a surprise.

Here's the real scoop. Don't take prophylaxis. Don't put yourself at risk of getting drug-resistant malaria. I had an engineer friend who died from Lariam-resistant malaria he picked up in Borneo. He had two relapses and a heart attack. End of story, literally.

Instead, my African friends recommended this Artemether, derived from wormwood. In 2002, it was only available as the Chinese herbal treatment. It is now available as a treatment from Novartis, a Swiss drug company that has combined it with an antiparasitical and called it Coartem.

Still, the best thing you do to prevent malaria is simple: Protect yourself at night. Use insect repellant, wear long sleeves and pants, and sleep under a mosquito (mozzie) net. I've spent well more than two years of my life in Africa, plus many months in New Guinea, Indonesia, Central and South America. So I estimate I've been in harm's way for more than four years total. I've never contracted malaria, likely due to my usual dumb luck and this simple step.

If you find yourself with a horrible headache and 104-degree fever, take Coartem immediately. Don't wait to be examined by a Western doctor and don't wait for a blood test. The way to cure malaria is to get the medicine in your system as soon as you suspect you have it. Coartem has no side effects, so if you've really contracted the flu you're not going to hurt yourself.

In two cases of malaria, one in Rome and the other in New York, acquaintances of mine died waiting for the results of the malaria test. I've also handed out Coartem to friends who have taken it and recovered completely within a week.

Don't bother to look for Coartem at your pharmacy. Don't ask your doctor for a prescription. The FDA hasn't approved the drug so you can't get it in the United States. Instead, go to a chemist in a Third World country and pick up a small cache. Like as not, they will sell you Coartem or Artemether without a prescription. If it costs you more than $15 for a four-day course of medication, you're being robbed.

I always keep at least two packets of Coartem with me. If Jackie and I split up during our travels (for example, she once flew to Paris from Harare while I stayed behind to work), we each carry a course of meds with us. The chances are you won't become symptomatic of malaria until you have left Africa for the First World—there is at least a fourteen-day incubation period—and the First World doesn't always accurately recognize malaria symptoms. If you come down with it in Africa, the doctors will treat you immediately. I guess what I'm saying is you're safer getting malaria in Africa than in the United States.

—

Mike and I concluded this trip in the Luangwa Valley in Zambia, trying to figure out how to keep the elephants that wouldn't stay in South Luangwa National Park from trampling the local communities' maize fields. We even explored the possibility of coating string fencing with a paste of oil and hot chili pepper. No kidding, elephants don't like the burning sensation of hot chili any more than the average human.

Our local project, working with the local Kunda tribe in a Game Management Area or GMA to develop a better-run hunting business, allowed us to test our theory. We instructed the locals to grow hot chili peppers as part of their row crops, grind up the chili harvest, and mix it with motor oil, then coat the double strand string fences with the bright red chili glop.

An elephant's trunk is an exquisitely complicated and sophisticated tool, made up of something like three hundred muscles. Elephants also have a highly developed sense of smell. If sticking habanero chili paste up your nose hurts, imagine what it must feel like to an elephant!

The chili experiment offered us another idea—to sell the unused portion of the harvest to the Tabasco folks. Unfortunately, the Luangwa Valley is too remote and the crop too small to make the exchange work.

While with the Kunda, I attended the annual meeting of their GMA association. I sat in the shade of a tree in the main village while they debated how to spend the net proceeds of the hunting operation. One fellow got up and gave a pitch for new football (soccer) uniforms. Finally, they decided among other distributions to give $12 US to every adult. I was transfixed. After the meeting, I cornered a WWF social scientist.

"What does this cash mean to the people of this tribe?" I asked.

"For about a quarter," he replied, "they can buy a meal out on the town. For another quarter, maybe pay their school fees. But, to half of these folks, the $24 is equal to about 60 percent of their annual cash income."

Wow!

We said good-bye at Lusaka International Airport. As I waited for my flight, I noticed that mechanics had the cowling off and were tinkering around with a jet engine at the gate right below the international lounge. Sure enough, it was my airplane.

By the time I landed in Johannesburg's Tambo International Airport, my connecting flight to the United States had already departed. I passed through customs and found the South African Airways desk.

I'll never be able to explain it, but SAA has the best flight crews of any airline—and the worst, most arrogant, ground staff. Naturally, the woman who "helped" me seemed to consider my plight an imposition. It took her awhile, but she finally found me a seat on a 747 leaving the following day *and* a room at the Holiday Inn that was within walking distance of the airport terminal. It was my lucky day.

The next morning, I took my time eating a terrific breakfast at the Holiday Inn. This Holiday Inn had a huge, wonderful buffet. I guess they felt the need to compete with "The Grace," an African family hotel chain that puts on the most amazing spread I ever saw. Imagine a solid silver, fish-shaped serving dish on which was served about 20 pounds of smoked salmon!

I finally walked over to the terminal to check in.

To my astonishment, a different blonde Afrikaans lady looked me straight in the eye and said, "You should have been here a lot earlier. You are on standby. I don't have a seat for you."

"Don't be ridiculous. I rebooked last night."

"No, you don't have a seat, blah, blah, blah."

"Please call your supervisor. Don't even think of arguing with me. Just do it," I demanded.

I got a middle seat in the last row on the airplane.

Earlier that year, Jackie and I had flown to Sydney, Australia. My wife struck up a conversation with a music executive from Chicago who sat across the aisle. Shortly after dinner was served, we observed that he fell asleep, practically drowning in his food. Twelve hours later, the stewardess had to shake him awake. "What on earth did you take to knock yourself out like that?" Jackie asked him. He reached in his shaving kit and handed her a little white pill. "Best stuff around," he said. "Works like a charm."

I looked it over. "Hmm. Ten milligram Valium," she noted. "That's about ten times the amateur dose. Promise me you'll break it in half if you ever need it." I dropped it into my travel kit.

So there I was in a middle seat with a nine-year-old girl next to me. Her parents were on the aisles. We took off. I turned on my movie screen. It didn't work. Awhile later, the crew bussed out the dinner trays. Five minutes later, the young lady fell asleep with her head on my shoulder.

I thought, *This is going to be a long flight.* Then I remembered that little white pill in my shaving kit. Without hesitation—not a fleeting thought to my children's future or my lovely wife—I popped the whole pill.

Fourteen hours later, the crew had to shake me awake. I stumbled off the airplane, mustered through customs and immigration. At least I think I did; I have no memory of doing so. I boarded a flight from Miami to Denver. I don't remember doing that either, but somehow I ended up at Denver International!

From that flight forward I've only flown business class, and only on planes that have beds.

CHAPTER 4

A Long Way from Anywhere

WE LEFT FROM CHARLES PRINCE Airport, the private field outside Harare. Charlie Mackie, our pilot, taxied ZWJE, the World Wildlife Fund Cessna 206, over to the little customs building where Mike Jones and I were waiting.

Half jokingly I asked, "How come this isn't 'Prince Charles' airport?'" I remind myself that I never got an answer, only a blank stare from the immigration guy.

When I entered Zimbabwe I had the forethought to ask immigration in Victoria Falls for a double entry visa, allowing me to travel into and out of Zim twice and saving me $15 US! The immigration guy at the airport stamped over a visa from a previous visit, but I didn't object—my passport is as cluttered as my garage at home. We loaded up the 206 for our three-hour flight to Lichinga, Mozambique.

Frankly, I marvel that I made this trip at all. When Mike invited me to visit the Sanga conservation area in Niassa Province, Mozambique, I mailed my passport off to the Mozambique embassy in Washington, DC, post haste. Those were the days when you couldn't get an "instant" visa at the port of entry. I hate sending away my passport, no matter the reason, and worry the whole time it is off somewhere. So, naturally, the Anthrax attacks of 2001 occurred the same day I mailed it off.

Ten days after I'd reluctantly dropped it in the post, someone knocked on my office door in LoDo (Lower Downtown). When I opened up, there stood Agent Rojo, all five feet two inches of her, in uniform, with what looked like a cannon in a holster on her hip.

"Mr. Warner?" she asked.

I nodded.

"I am a postal inspector. Do you know anything about a package with your return address on it?" She described the package.

"Oh no," I groaned. "My passport is in that package. It's going to the Embassy of Mozambique in Washington."

I convinced her that the package was completely innocent and that I had not put any anthrax spores in with my passport.

"It was found in a drop box in Windsor, Colorado," Agent Rojo explained.

"How the devil did it get there? Do I have to go to Windsor to retrieve it? Can I get it back?"

"Let's call Sandy Magley in Windsor," Agent Rojo suggested.

We called the postmistress in Windsor, described the package, and confirmed it hadn't been tampered with. She promised to express it the same day.

Of course that wasn't the end of it. The next day I emailed the embassy and followed up with a phone call. They promised to move the visa along. Unfortunately, upon completion, they dropped it in the mail instead of FedExing it to me as I had requested. The postal facilities in Washington were still getting bleached to kill any remaining anthrax spores, holding up the mail significantly.

Day by day I watched the mail for the passport that didn't come. Thank God it showed up the day before I was scheduled to leave, proving correct once again what James Bond said in *Casino Royale*: "Worry is a dividend paid to disaster before it is due."

You should have seen my travel bag by the time I was ready to leave for the airport: It was full of items unavailable in Zimbabwe that I was bringing in for friends. My days as a smuggler had begun. There was a GPS unit for Russell, a digital camera for Deb, and a new computer for Mike. There were clothes, binoculars, watches—all gifts for friends or friends-of-friends. I packed my own binoculars and, of course, fishing gear for Mike and me. There was no room left for clothes. Thankfully safari clothes are easy: I packed two pairs of zip-off leg pants and a few shirts, and I shoved socks and underwear anywhere there was a spot.

As Murphy's Law would have it, I was informed at the airport in Miami that I had been randomly selected for a baggage search. They escorted me to a little room where a South African golfer who had been in the States for a PGA tournament was being searched. The inspector was picking his luggage apart with the proverbial fine-tooth comb. After about fifteen minutes even the airline personnel were getting agitated.

Finally a Delta Airlines attendant blurted out, "It's a golf ball, for goodness sake," referring to the round white object the security agent was scrutinizing like it was a bomb.

About that moment I resolved that there was no way I would make my plane. I could predict the scenario: the inspectors would open my bag and then open every package in it. They'd detain me for trying to sneak goods through customs and I'd be stuck.

As I was envisioning the worst-case scenario an airline agent walked up to where I was sitting and said, "Your bag was cleared." It didn't really register. I sat there for another five minutes.

The same guy walked back in and looked at me. "Why are you still here?" he asked. "You're clear to go."

I ran like hell to make my plane.

Just as I pitched up at the gate, I heard an announcement: "These passengers will please line up for a search of carry-on luggage."

My name was fourteen out of fifteen. If I had waited to line up in numerical order, I never would have made my flight. So, I did what any sane person would do: I grabbed my backpack, leapt over a railing, and elbowed my way to second in line.

You know, I never did see that golfer get on the plane. Did they X-ray his golf balls after all?

The flight from Miami to Johannesburg is about fourteen hours. The return flight is sixteen hours. In my opinion, the only way to endure the trip is with pharmaceuticals and cocktails—my personal favorite combination is whiskey and Ambien. The trick to beating jet lag is to figure out which eight-hour period you will be sleeping at your destination and take a pill that will knock you out for the corresponding time while on the airplane. Works like a charm. I almost never suffer from jet lag.

Before going on to Mozambique, Mike and I stopped in Harare for a day. I wanted to deliver presents for a friend's sister. Talk about six degrees of separation: a great friend of mine, Daniel Neufeld, fell in love late in life with a woman, Elizabeth Gundlach, whose sister, Deb, has lived in Zimbabwe since getting out of the Peace Corps in the seventies. She went to work for the intensely feared Central Intelligence Organisation (CIO), or secret police. Believe me, I keep her phone number at hand when traveling across Zim.

So, there we were off to Lichinga, Mozambique. We flew northeast across eastern Zimbabwe, crossed Malawi, and landed at the biggest, emptiest airport I'd ever seen. During the flight, I noticed that we didn't fly a straight line. We were flying a leg that skirted Zambian airspace.

I asked Charlie over the radio, "How come we're going around Zambia?"

Charlie's answer was only semi-amusing: "The Zambian Air Force has a tendency to shoot at anything in its airspace."

On the approach to Lichinga, I got a good look at the airport from the air. It looked as big as La Guardia! The runway was sixteen thousand feet long. Even from the air, the airport looked brand new.

The airport had everything—except airplanes. The passenger terminal had everything—except passengers. Simon Astey, our grad student contact, and Tony Abucar, our Conservation Department contact, picked us up and delivered us to Tony's boss—the provincial minister—who had flown all the way up from Maputo, the capital, a thousand miles to the south. Simon went off to find the customs agent who needed to stamp our passports. The customs agent wasn't at the airport when we arrived. But you could hardly fault him for not being on the job—there not actually being a job to do.

Remember that hard-won visa? Forty minutes later Simon returned to the minister's office. I saw his face and knew there was trouble.

"The customs officer refused to stamp your passports. He desires all of you to fly to Tete—about two hours away by air—to enter the country 'legally.'"

Or, I thought, *Simon could've offered him a bribe but he knew we wouldn't have wanted him to do that.*

Tony translated for the minister. His embarrassment was palpable.

"You are guests of my country," he stammered in Portuguese. "I will prepare letters of credential under which you will travel." *Thank you, Mr. Minister, sir.*

Lichinga is a nice little frontier town. The main streets, all two of them, are paved. In fact, the town was full of new SUVs of various denominations. Most had roll bars and oversized tires. All were four-wheel drive. If you saw what constituted a road in Niassa, you wouldn't think the town was overrun with suburban housewives.

We stayed overnight at Quinta Capricornio, just a kilometer north of town, run by two scruffy women. One was Dutch, the other Scottish. After just a short time, I decided they were pretty damn okay for a couple of expat farmers. They served meals in a "rondel" type open-air building. The tables were wedge shaped and we sat on benches. That evening as we ate dinner and drank beer, we were joined by a well-dressed couple, apparently out on the town. The farm had a pet bush pig. He was quite tame, but demanded a certain amount of attention from the guests.

The guest at the other table did her best to ignore the pig when it came in during dinner. It snuffled up behind her expecting to be scratched on the head. (Try scratching a bristle brush and you'll get the idea). The pig pushed against her a couple of times. She fended it off with her pretty little white shoe. (It's amazing the details you record in your memory without intending to!) The pig apparently felt rejected. It stuck its snout under the bench and lifted up. The poor woman went flying halfway across the table. That was one mighty pig! The Scotswoman fended off the pig with a broom, but when it returned later and snuffled up to my table I gave it a good scratch!

The next day we were to fly off to Sanga. Simon had arranged for the local people to clear an old Portuguese airstrip adjacent to a fort abandoned in 1975. I elected to drive with Simon while Charlie, Mike, and Tony flew. Always the geologist, I wanted to see the ground close up. Instead of an hour's flight we had an eight-hour drive. And that was on a good road!

Simon, the two game scouts, and I drove through miombo forest and rolling hills. The kopjes, small elevations that rise from an otherwise flat area, were with the typical African granite-topped knobs. As we neared the first village we saw a procession of people walking along the edge of the road, escorting a dead man laid out on a plank. We learned that one of the chief's sons had been bitten by a black mamba—one of the most aggressive and highly venomous snakes—while working in a maize field that morning. He had died from the bite.

We camped at the abandoned Portuguese fort, where a twin-engine bomber had been shot up while trying to land on a taxiway during the War of Independence. When I saw it, I realized what a job the locals had done clearing the airstrip for us. There were big trees growing through the remains of fuselage. The fort was not quite as shot up as the airplane. The Portuguese, who controlled much of the area from the sixteenth century, had abandoned the fort shortly after the first and only battle. We slept in a partly collapsed building. I noticed that my cot was kinda surrounded by the others. Charlie winked at me. "Can't let the donor get eaten by a hyena, I reckon."

We sat around a fire that night, eating what the team called a "Portuguese bush dinner" of spaghetti and beans. I can't say what's particularly Portuguese about this meal, but who am I to argue? After we'd passed around the bottle of scotch a few times, Charlie Mackie told us a story.

Charlie, like Mike, had been a Rhodesian National Parks ranger. He had been out on patrol one Sunday morning. From the Land Rover, he and his game scouts spotted quite fresh human footprints.

"We couldn't tell whether they were in front or behind us, so we gave it a guess and decided to turn around, back the way we came. Two minutes later we were hit by an RPG."

RPGs, or rocket-propelled grenades, were a weapon of choice during the War of Independence, also known as the "Bush War," when nationalists fought to regain control of the then-Southern Rhodesian government of Ian Smith.

"It hit just below the windscreen on the passenger side of the Land Rover, just forward of where I was sitting—blew me up pretty good. My guts were doing their level best to fall out. Another bloke had a head wound. Blood everywhere, but in fact his wound was superficial—mine was anything but. The other two scouts dragged us out and sat us behind a leadwood tree. Pretty good cover, but the other side [the nationalists] had AK-47s. We only had two H & H .375 magnums. Not a fair matchup. My bloke got on the radio and called in. Trouble was, it was Sunday and the main office was closed. The standby was on a low-power receiver and the girl couldn't understand us."

Charlie couldn't help but indulge in a little British understatement. "Maybe it was the shouting combined with the gunfire [that finally got a response]. I got nicked by rifle fire, through the hip. I really thought I was done for. Finally, one of the other blokes walked into the office and heard the commotion on the radio. He ran to the main office and was able to contact us. He called in the attack helicopter. We got out all right.

"Came out of the dustup okay, you know. Got me to hospital and sewed my middle up. Bullet through the hip seemed to miss most everything important. Only regret is the loss of sight in my left eye."

"You're blind in one eye?" I asked, astonished.

"Yep."

"Hell, I've got a one-eyed pilot," I mused out loud. Everybody laughed—and it wasn't the scotch.

"Don't need but one eye to see the instruments, you know." The truth is Charlie is a damn fine pilot, and a mighty fine storyteller, too.

"Charlie," I said, "you should write your stories up and get them published."

"Already been done, Ed," Charlie responded. "Book called *Sometimes When It Rains*" (by Keith Meadows, Thorntree Press, 2000)."

—

The next night Charlie related how he acquired his Piper Super Cub, a small, single-engine bush plane. One of Charlie's many areas of expertise is aerial game counting. No, you don't have to point out that he has one eye. A pilot doesn't have to look at the instruments all the time, you know. On a job over the Congo when the International Union for Conservation of Nature (IUCN) attempted, unsuccessfully, a game count of forest elephants, he spotted the "remains" of an airplane in a clearing in the forest. Noting the location on the GPS, he went on with his count. A week later, with some time off, he decided to try to locate the wreck on the ground. It took two days of driving around on bush tracks to finally get to the site. The plane had been successfully landed in a small opening . . . well, mostly successfully. It would take some work to patch it up, but who could do that better than Charlie? He drove into town, where he inquired about a lost Super Cub. Hearing that no one had ever reported it, he ordered parts. He was going to rebuild the plane, but realized that the clearing was too small even for a Super Cub to take off. So what to do?

He removed the wings, loaded the fuselage and wings onto a lorry, and drove it to the nearest clearing large enough for takeoff (five hundred feet is plenty!). Charlie put the plane back together again, cleared the brush, and flew it to Kampala (probably to refuel and go through customs) and then home. It's now parked at Charles Prince Airport in Harare ready for Charlie when he needs it. I saw it on our return from Mozambique. You couldn't find a prettier little plane.

The next morning we decided to do a nonscientific game count of the Sanga area. We piled into the WWF Cessna 206, with Mike up front. Mike's prosthesis makes it hard for him to sit in tight spots. Remember? While working for Parks, he stepped on a land mine at Mana Pools. These Parks guys are tough! Two Mozambiquan game scouts joined us in the plane, so I was stuffed in the far back-left corner. Off we went, flying the usual two hundred to three hundred feet off the deck.

All around me the guys were calling off animal sightings in English and Portuguese. Every once in a while I managed to spot an animal myself. I shouted, "Antelope, nine o'clock—size of a dog," but honestly I had no idea what I'd seen. In hindsight, I'm almost certain it was a dik dik (which is technically an antelope!). After about twenty minutes and a hundred sightings, I actually recognized the sable antelope Charlie spotted. My eyes were finally starting to discern the differences in the landscape.

As we flew northward toward the Ruva River and the Tanzanian border, we began to see elephant tracks. Even I couldn't mistake elephant tracks! They are big and round. All of a sudden, off to the left, I spotted a watering hole and three "big" animals with their heads down drinking water.

I shouted, "Elephant, three!" Charlie threw the 206 into a tight turn back to the site and everyone scanned for elephants. Around we went— and then around again.

Finally, Charlie shouted to me, "Where did you see the elephant?"

"At that pan we passed to port," I replied confidently.

With great British sarcasm Charlie informed me, "Ed, those were bush pigs."

I sat in the back and kept my mouth shut the rest of the flight. Elephants indeed! I would hear about this for the rest of the trip if I didn't do something.

We landed half an hour later at the old military airstrip. Driving back to camp in the Land Cruiser, I spotted three bull elephants a hundred yards from the track. "Bush pigs, three!" I shouted at the top of my lungs. Simon slammed on the brakes and we all bailed out, running after the bulls. I followed the two game scouts as the team split up: I figured that they knew what they were doing. I wasn't so sure of the other two mzungus. We managed to get within 150 yards, but the bulls weren't habituated to humans and wouldn't let us get close. Running toward the elephants, I managed to get stabbed by a burned grass stem. I now sport a little tattoo on my ankle to commemorate the event.

Later that afternoon we met with four village chiefs. The fifth couldn't make the three-day walk after crossing a crocodile-infested river—and his village doesn't have a boat. The meeting was conducted in Yao (a Bantu language) translated into Portuguese and then into English and back again. I wasn't directly involved so I began to get a little distracted. The village kids all came down to watch the proceedings. I wanted desperately to take a picture of one beautiful young girl, about six years old, wearing a dress that came only to her midsection. But manners in that part of the world demand permission and I couldn't interrupt the meeting for a request like that. Another photo op down the drain.

I also noticed a young girl, maybe eleven, based on her androgynous shape, with a baby on her hip. I thought to myself, *How nice, the older daughter is helping her mom.* What an idiot! I found out later the baby was hers.

During the meeting with the chiefs, the conversation shifted to government help with the locals' wild bee keeping. Their custom is to use bark hives, but the government had given them box-shaped hives with instructions to manufacture them. I gathered from the conversation that the box hive didn't work worth a damn. Charlie tried to tell them how to fix the box, but I could see that the chiefs didn't find his explanation worth a damn, either.

Finally, Charlie said to the translator, "Tell the chiefs that I keep bees myself and have done so for thirty years."

Oh! The chiefs looked at each other. I swear they raised their eyebrows. They asked Charlie a few questions to be sure he really was an apiarist. The next thing I know, we're hoofin' it through the bush to look at their beehives.

One of the questions asked of the chiefs was why their school was in such a state of disrepair. The chiefs explained that schooling was a plot foisted on them by Christian missionaries, the real object of which was to convert their children from Islam to Christianity. I would have liked to argue that education was valuable for its own sake, but from the tribe's experience their story was hard to discount. One of the unintended negative consequences of missionary work in the area is the forced marriage of girls at younger and younger ages—an effort to keep them tied more completely to customs of the village and lessen the effect of Western education. Thus, the barely pubescent girl carrying the baby.

After several days in the bush we flew back to Zimbabwe, stopping for fuel at Lichinga then crossing western Mozambique, Lake Niassa, Malawi (skirting Zambia, of course), and back to Harare.

Customs agents (probably cousins of Robert Mugabe) searched every square inch of the Cessna. They were greatly concerned about a couple of gallons of water Charlie had stashed in the rear of the Cessna. After a short period of harassment, he invited them to drink it. They let us go. And no, they didn't drink the water.

If you don't think the Zim government is paranoid, I refer you to "Zimbabwe Reports Seizing Plane With 64 Suspected Mercenaries," an article in the *New York Times* (March 9, 2004). A private rafting party were arrested on suspicion of being "American government mercenaries" and tossed in jail. That very easily could have happened to us.

My only regret is having to return the "letter of credential" to the provincial minister. I would have liked to keep it as a souvenir. Seems he was a proponent of "leave no trace."

—

Before leaving Zimbabwe, I dropped down to Vic Falls to visit my friends, Russell and Leanne.

Russell had recently moved from the Gwayi Conservancy, where his in-laws own a game ranch adjoining Hwange National Park, to Victoria Falls with Leanne and their two young kids. They had invited me to stay with them, but I didn't know what kind of place they'd rented and didn't want to impose, so I booked a room at the famous, old Victoria Falls Hotel. Russell picked me up, and on the way, Russell explained a recent government edict concerning foreigners and hotel rooms.

"You have to pay in US dollars at the official exchange rate," he told me. I thought about this for ten seconds.

"You mean that I pay at $1 US to $55 Zim while the bank rate is around $1 US to $200 Zim and the black market is $1 US to $250 Zim?" Sure enough, the hotel wanted $575 US for a night's stay.

"So, about that invitation to stay with you guys?" I said.

My eyes opened to the highway robbery, Russell and I figured out a system. Russell would pay my expenses in Zim dollars and I would reimburse him in US dollars.

Russell conveyed some bad news from Mike: Rain had fallen in the upper Zambezi basin and the river was muddy. No tigerfishing at Sedinda Lodge! The water was too muddy for the fish to see the lures.

"How about Lake Kariba?" Russell proposed. "I'll fix you up with a houseboat!"

"Now, Ed," he continued, admonishing me, "you can't be an American. You blokes get the worst deals. Let's make you South African."

"Righto, mate," I said enthusiastically.

"Hmm," Russell thought out loud, "you probably shouldn't open your mouth at any rate. I'll make a phone call."

We got a houseboat for twelve at the cost of $125 US per night, instead of $350 (the going rate for American tourists). I only wish I could have filled the thing.

Mike Jones came down from Harare and joined me for a few days of R&R. Mike and I had a crew of three. It might have been romantic if we'd had ladies aboard to share our dinners on the deck (and if we didn't have to spit out the bugs that flew into our mouths with every other bite of food). Still, I caught my first tigerfish, the biggest of the trip at 8 pounds. When it took the line, I swear I thought I'd snared a tree stump. That is until the fish jumped. Tigerfish look like a cross between a large mouth bass and a barracuda. They're ugly, but there's no mistaking them.

6.5 kg tigerfish caught on the Caprivi Strip by me
(looking exhausted for a reason). Come on folks, all work and no play??

In thanks for Russell's help, I took his family out for dinner at the Safari Lodge—the most expensive in Victoria Falls. The dinner bill was $16,000 Zim. I gave Russell eighty bucks, letting him decide if he wanted to exchange the US dollars at his bank for $16,000 Zim or get the black market rate of at least $20,000 Zim. I estimate the cost of that meal for three was somewhere between $55 and $275 US. I love to watch the market at work.

—

When I arrived back in Denver I called the Tattered Cover Book Store to order *Sometimes When It Rains*. It arrived four months later—just about average for surface mail between the United States and Africa.

CHAPTER 5

On the Road with Russell

THROUGH 2003 AND 2004, MY wife and I built a home. We bought a property in order to build our dream house: Frank Lloyd Wright meets the twenty-first century. The trouble is I made an unfortunate promise: I would stay home until construction of the house was finished.

We were living in a wonderful townhouse in the Cherry Creek neighborhood of Denver, an area in which you can walk to shops, a mall, and restaurants. Our new property was only seven blocks east of our townhouse, so we could walk or bike to the site during building. After many months of revisions to the architectural plans, construction finally began. With weekly meetings with our contractor and architect, the project started to look like it would never be finished. I was getting blue.

One day I returned home to our townhouse to find that the cleaning guy had broken the glass off a group of little watercolor paintings Jackie had made of African scenes. (He had an unfortunate habit of breaking things; fortunately—at least for him—my wife is loyal beyond patience.) The grouping was made up of three painted scenes: a sunset through dead trees over Lake Kariba; a white-throated bee-eater with a fly in its mouth; and, a line of bluish-purple elephants. The fourth piece in the group was a preserved sprig of Botswana sage. With the glass broken, the house was filled with the smell of the sage—the smell of the Kalahari Desert.

Jackie, seeing the look on my face as I took in the scent, said, "Go. Just go. Get outta here and go to Africa."

—

During the nine months of self-imposed grounding, the Sand County Foundation had been pestering me to return to Africa and to our shared projects. They wanted me to go fact-finding and to do a series of interviews of stakeholders involved in conservation. I was to travel to Zimbabwe and Zambia to interview NGO scientists and government officials, national park game wardens and private landowners. There was just one minor hurdle to overcome: The Zimbabwean government had banned Western journalists.

Not a problem. I had already discovered the perfect cover for my SCF and smuggling adventures. I'd come off the plane in safari khakis with a camera around my neck and a goofy grin on my face. I would tell anyone within hearing how happy I was to be back, how I loved the country, and what kind of safari I was going on, walking, driving, or as you'll see later on, biking my way across the African savanna. When arriving in Africa, never check "business," always check "tourist" on your entry documents, and play the returning tourist who is so in love with the culture you just couldn't stay away. Under my cover I could both smuggle and conduct interviews and build relationships. My acting skills allowed me to do things that most people would never consider doing. There's a bravery (perhaps foolish) that comes with the skill of acting.

Why bother, you ask?

Well, smuggling just may be one of my true callings. Each trip I would bring in computers, GPS units, cameras, transmitters, receivers, binoculars, aircraft parts, scientific equipment, and much more for my colleagues. You name it, I've smuggled it. The customs duties, necessary bribes, and delayed paperwork are so onerous that I could circumvent months of delays and tens of thousands of dollars of costs to the research groups. I once smuggled twelve leopard teeth back into the States, delivering them to a wildlife expert in Wyoming. Naturally, I carried the teeth in my pants pocket.

This particular trip required considerable logistical preparation. I was going to be driving for three weeks across two countries, staying with friends, camping in national parks, and visiting safari lodges. Things were very bad in Zimbabwe in 2003. Mugabe and his thugs had stolen their second election in 2002, the economy had collapsed, hyperinflation was rampant, the roads were increasingly dangerous, and there were no rental cars or fuel to be had in Zim.

No problem! I called my friend Russell Gammon, and hired him to be my traveling companion, translator, and security contingent.

Russell—the guy who carries a 500 Nitro Express like I'd carry a .22—began arranging our trip. He found a Land Cruiser that I could rent from a family friend for a mere $2,000 cash, in US hundred-dollar bills. He then secured an import permit for two barrels of diesel, picked them up in Kasane, Botswana, across the border from Victoria Falls, where he and his family live. He then drove one barrel partway across the country to his father-in-law's place on the Gwayi Conservancy to stash it.

I love bizarre connections—six degrees of separation and all that—don't you? Just before I left for Africa, I was talking to Karen Cockburn of Africa Travel Centre, the agency in Boulder that has handled some of my Africa trips. Karen's husband, Brian, was Zimbabwean, and Karen, an American, had lived in Zim for years. I asked Karen where I should stay in Bulawayo, where I was to connect with Russell. There used to be plenty of Air Zim flights but only two were left on the schedule and it looked like I had to fly in at night.

Karen said, "Why don't you stay with my best girlfriend, Deidre Adams, and her husband, Gomez?"

Deidre had been married to Brian's cousin, who was killed in a plane crash in the bush. *That Cockburn family must be cursed*, I thought, reminding myself, sadly, that Brian had died in an auto accident. Deidre remarried this character, Derek "Gomez" Adams (as in "Gomez Addams" of *The Addams Family* TV show).

"In fact," Karen went on, "I talked to her a couple of days ago. She just had a baby."

I mulled over her suggestion for a few seconds.

"Hey, Karen, I've got an idea. Why don't I deliver a present from you to Deidre and Gomez for the new baby. I don't want to stay with them— Deidre has her hands full, I'm sure, but a present from Karen delivered by some unknown Yank would be a kick in the pants. I'll come up to Boulder for my plane tickets. You have a present wrapped. Give me their phone number and I'll be your delivery boy!"

I arrived in Harare a week later. I've already mentioned how lucky I am. Try this little experience on for size. As I mentioned a little earlier, my second most important work in Africa is as a smuggler. I always show up with electronic equipment since the added cost plus duties jack the price up about 300 percent. This trip, in my checked luggage, I had a new laptop, camera, and GPS. In my carry-on I had my own laptop, camera, binoculars, and digital recorder. My connecting flight between Jo'burg and Harare was just an hour. When I got off the plane in Harare, I noticed (being a trained observer and all) two interesting facts: I was the only American going through customs and when we got to the baggage claim the South African Airways rep was already standing there waiting to inform us that our baggage hadn't made the flight (you guessed it, overseas baggage never makes that one-hour connection). I was pulled out of the "Nothing to Declare" line by the customs lady, likely another paranoid cousin of Robert Mugabe. She went through my carry-on luggage with a fine-tooth comb. The customs search was a minor delay. I was really concerned about what would happen the next day when my smuggled goods arrived.

The last item pulled out of my carry-on was my digital recorder. "What's this?" the customs officer asked.

"Oh, that's my new digital recorder," I replied, offhandedly. In a flash, I remembered that members of the Western press had been banned from Zim. *Oops!* Suspicion clouded her face.

"What are you going to use this for?" she inquired.

"Well," I screwed up my face into that goofy tourist grin, "I'm going on a two-week private safari, and I want to record the adventures, you know, all the sounds of animals I meet along the way."

Another customs agent walked up. "Is that really expensive?" he asked. I swallowed hard. If you're going to act like a dumb tourist, you might as well go all the way. "Sure is," I replied. "Cost me over two hundred fifty bucks US."

Mugabe's cousin looked at the other agent, looked at me grinning stupidly, looked at the recorder wistfully, and tossed it back in my backpack. She filled out a form requiring me to return to customs the next day with my checked bag.

"You can go now," she said imperiously.

I returned the next day to claim my delayed bag—the one full of contraband. I scanned the terminal and spotted a group of four well-dressed black Zimbabweans. I rolled my bag over and struck up a conversation. Together, we walked around customs and exited the airport.

I stayed a couple of nights with Mike and Mary Ann in Harare. We invited a couple of people out to dinner at the most expensive steak house in town. That day, the value of the Zim dollar went through one of its periodic crashes, dropping 400 percent instantly. So, when I picked up the menu and saw the previous day's prices, I had an epiphany. I called over the owner of the restaurant and asked him to change a US fifty-dollar bill so I could pay in local currency. He got the new rate on the street. I paid the bill and filled my backpack with Zim five-hundred-dollar notes. The meal cost twenty bucks and the remainder was exactly what I needed for three weeks of travel. That is, just so long as I could keep my mouth shut when paying bills. If anyone suspected I was a Yank the price would go up 1,000 percent!

After conducting interviews with scientists affiliated with World Wildlife Fund and the Resilience Alliance, Mike dropped me off at the airport for my evening trip to Bulawayo.

Delivery Boy

There was nothing to do or see in the domestic gate lounge of Harare airport. The whole airport was as empty as a tomb—it was spooky. There were a few well-dressed Zimbabweans, but what caught my attention was a family. There was a mum and dad and three kids who ranged in age from about ten to fourteen. One of the girls wore an athletic jacket that said "Bulawayo Gymnastics." Not surprisingly, they were waiting for the flight I had booked. With nothing else to do, I eavesdropped on their conversation. After a few minutes of chitchat, the teenage girl in the jacket said something to her "mum." In her reply, the mother said something about "Deidre." I was instantly curious. Deidre's not the most common name. So, I got up and walked over to the group.

"Excuse me, but I couldn't help overhear your conversation. Do you know a woman named Deirdre Adams, by any chance?" They all started talking at once. The father was another of Brian's cousins, a brother to Deirdre's first husband killed in the plane crash. The teenage girl was Deidre's daughter from her first marriage, in Harare for a gymnastics competition.

"Would you like me to call Deidre on the telly for you?" asked the woman. "The family will be at the airport to pick up Moozi here."

"Don't call. I've got an idea. Hey Moozi, you game for a joke? Let's walk out of baggage arm-in-arm, with me holding the present for your little sister."

What a great kid. She didn't know me from Adam (or Gomez), but eagerly agreed.

We passed through the baggage room door in the Bulawayo airport. Standing in the lounge was the whole Adams family: Deidre, Gomez, their son, and a very young, red-faced baby. Moozi and I walked up to them. I expected astonishment.

"Hi, Ed," said Deidre. "Welcome to Bulawayo. Thanks for escorting Nicole [aka Moozi] through the airport. We'll expect you for tea tomorrow morning at nine."

"How'd you know?" I sputtered.

There, standing off to one side of the family, was Russell. His expression quickly turned from ear-to-ear grin to the classic hangdog expression when he realized my disappointment in being scooped.

Naturally, he knew the family. All the Zim safari guides know one another. They'd been chatting about me while they had waited for the plane to arrive. Oh, well. Getting one over on these Zimbos ain't easy.

Russell and I arrived at the Adams residence the next morning for tea. Gomez had the biggest damned tigerfish on his wall, stuffed and mounted, of course. Then and there I became even more fascinated by these toothy monsters. I resolved not to return to Africa without fishing tackle again.

CHAPTER 6

The Gwayi

RUSSELL AND I DROVE THROUGH the Lowveld from Bulawayo eastward to the banks of the Save River, just to the west of the Mozambique border. We encountered many roadblocks along the way— you know, the kind manned by "police" armed with AK-47s. That particular weekend, it turned out, was the "Heroes and Ancestors" national holiday. (Irreverent as ever, Zimbos sometimes called it "Gooks and Spooks.") Every stop, Russell would chat up the cops (or army dudes) in an accent and cadence of speech that was very different from how he spoke to me. Finally, I had to ask.

"Naw, Ed, you must be mistaken," he drawled in that modification of a British accent that the Brits think is "low class," but Americans find charming. "You better keep to the shade for a coupla days."

An hour later, we hit the next roadblock.

"Good day, chaps," said Russell. "Baggin' any drunks along the tar this mornin'?"

We drove on. Russell looked over at me. His eyebrows were raised.

"You're a pretty observant fellow, Ed."

"Oh," I drawled back at him, "that was you talking, not some other chap?"

—

As you might imagine, I get some flak from friends and relatives about my Third World travels. They worry that something bad might happen to me. My stock rejoinder is "The most dangerous thing I do in life is drive on a Colorado highway." In hindsight, it's maybe not the most dangerous, at least compared to traveling along African roads where, if you aren't arrested at a roadblock, you'll likely hit a pothole big enough to swallow a Volkswagen bus.

We drove from Bulawayo to Russell's in-laws' place on the Gwayi. We were met at the gate by his father-in-law Chris Van Wyk (pronounced Van Veck) and the meanest, ugliest dog I ever saw. It must have been a cross between a bulldog and the demon-dog from *Ghostbusters.* It immediately ran up to me, put its paws on my shoulders, and licked my face.

"Nice monster," I said. "Glad to know you, please don't bite me."

We stayed the night with the family, descendants of the Boers, including two brothers-in-law, both professional hunters, and Russell's mother-in-law. The Boers are descendants of the Dutch settlers of Southern Africa during the eighteenth and nineteenth centuries. For the first time in my life, I was uncomfortable in someone's home. I can't explain exactly why, but I just felt uneasy.

The Van Wyks spoke mostly English, but that didn't make me feel any more comfortable. Even if they had been speaking Afrikaans (a degraded form of Dutch), which I love to hear and try to winkle out what's being said, I still would have felt the discomfort. There was a negative energy, even though they were trying to be polite to their guest. I can only imagine it stems from a cultural history of disliking English-speaking people. Still, I'm not entirely sure if it was dislike of Russell and his family history or if it was cultural baggage or both.

I've stayed in the homes of the rich and famous. I've spent nights wandering around Harare chatting up folks on the street and in the *shebeens.* I've slept in a *boma* in an African village. I've slept rough, in the elements. I've never been as uncomfortable around anyone before this experience.

There was just something about this family that made me uneasy—a gut feeling, if you will.

We departed for Gonarezhou National Park the next day. Midmorning, I mentioned to Russell my discomfort of the night before.

He started laughing. "Ed, let me tell you a little story that happened early in my relationship with Leanne."

"Chris's ancestors were on the Great Trek, when the Boers left the Cape Colony for the Transvaal. They hated the Brits then and they don't feel all too kindly to them today. Remember, I'm of British descent. Even worse, I'm a Meikles descendent on my mother's side—Scots traders who crossed the Transvaal all the way to the Zambezi, forging the way for British colonial expansion. So, there I was at a funeral with Leanne. Her cousins spoke to me in Afrikaans the whole time. It's not just that they wouldn't speak English—I knew that they're fluent. No, they spoke Afrikaans the whole time and talked about me as if I wasn't there."

To the Boers, "Meikles" represents the worst of British colonial expansionism. Russell, though, refused to join the family business. He wanted to be more like the Boers—living out in the wild and immersed in the natural world.

"I guess they used the language to exclude you because you're an outsider?" I proposed.

In typical "British" understatement, Russell agreed. "It was the height of rudeness, and I was offended."

CHAPTER 7

Gonarezhou National Park and the Southeast Lowveld

I INTERVIEWED THE GAME WARDEN for Gonarezhou National Park when we arrived at Chipinda Pool, camp headquarters. He didn't seem to mind that I used my little digital recorder. I asked him pointedly about poaching by National Parks game rangers.

He didn't even hesitate. "Oh, yes, our staff has to eat, you know."

What he did object to was my attempt to pay my camping fee in Zim dollars. He insisted on US and when I didn't have a small enough note, he smacked his lips and said, "So sorry, we can't make change." Not in US or in Zim currency. The campsite cost me $20 instead of $5. Good thing I had a few twenties stashed along with all those hundred-dollar bills.

We camped on the banks of the Runde River. As we were about to get out of the truck, an enormous bull elephant came out of the woods and flapped his massive ears, creating a dust cloud as he took a few steps toward us.

Gonarezhou elephant, just before he crashed into a fallen tree preventing
him from coming through the side of the Land Cruiser in 2006.

Russell started up the truck and drove on. "Gonas elephants are the most aggressive around," he explained. "The Shangaans [a Zulu people] became the best ivory poachers in Southern Africa—even better than the Zambians. The most famous of them was Shadrek, a wily fellow who lived in the park for years, holed up in the hollow of a baobab tree, and couldn't be caught. He shot the elephants in this park for years. They have never forgotten. I'd rather move than camp near that big fellow. He just might decide to stomp us into paste."

We pulled up to Fishans, a campsite on the second bench above the Runde River. The campsite had a concrete grill, a big stone fire ring, and an outhouse that looked doubtful at best. We pitched camp, broke out the beer, and cooked dinner. I wandered a short distance from camp in search of a "lava tree."

Have you heard the African joke, "How many types of trees do you find in Africa? Three: firewood, shade tree, and 'lava tree.'" Get it?

I walked on back after relieving myself. There, on the camp table, was a birthday cake (actually a big old elephant turd). It had a candle in the middle, and a bottle of scotch beside it.

"Good enough for me," I said to Russell. "You start cutting the cake. I'm gonna start drinkin' the scotch."

Amazingly, I would be stuck at this same campsite on another trip. Small world, considering Gonarezhou National Park is more than one-and-a-quarter-million acres.

I needed a bath, but I was not going to bathe in an African river. The Nile crocodiles might be hungry. So I stared into the water along the river's edge until I thought my eyes were going pop, stripped naked except for my Tevas, ran to the river, filled a bucket, and darted back up the shore about twenty-five meters, my dangly bits flappin' in the breeze. Home again, home again, jiggity, jig!

CHAPTER 8

The Save Valley Conservancy

I HAVE BEEN ATTACKED BY a big old bear, swum with
an eighteen-foot hammerhead shark, and been chased into thick acacia
thorn bush by a black rhino. But the most dangerous situation I've ever
been in was driving too fast on a dirt road through the Save Valley Conservancy.

We were visiting Weldon and Kathy Schenck, South Carolinians who
fell in love with Zimbabwe in the midnineties and bought Hammond
Ranch, located just inside the southern border of the Save Valley Conservancy.

The Schenck's ranch lies directly south of Clive Stockil's Senuko
Ranch. They border on the Nyangombi community and maintain good
relations, having supported the Nyangombi primary school and helped
develop an embroidery craft business for the Nyangombi women.

Kathy Schenck is descended from a signer of the Declaration of
Independence. Or was it the US Constitution? Either way, you get the
picture. Kathy's brother owns a bank. Weldon is a self-made man, having run Sara Lee's operation overseas. They own a ranch in the South
Carolina low country, where they raise Tennessee walking horses. I'm
sure most everything Weldon has touched has turned to gold. They were

bitten by the Africa bug but can't let go of the Old South. They have lived in South Carolina for a coon's age and don't appear ready to leave, even though they love Africa and would like to relocate there permanently.

The Schencks bought Hammond Ranch from Sam Levi, the most notorious businessman in Zimbabwe. Levi sold Hammond to the Schencks for the highest per acre price ever received for a piece of the Zimbabwean desert. Sam's daughter, a lawyer, handled the transaction, and as legend has it, after all was finalized, she came back to the Schencks and explained that they would have to pay for the cattle that remained on the ranch or have the mombies (cows) transferred to another Levi ranch. Kathy and Weldon had fallen in love, so they did whatever was necessary to get their hands on Hammond.

I was in business once upon a time. The first rule I learned was *never let the buyer (or seller) know how badly you want it.* Go to acting school and learn to dissimulate. Learn to put on a poker face. Whatever you do, don't let your opponent know what's in your hand. The Schencks, bless their souls, didn't know the first thing about negotiating.

Don't get me wrong. I love the Schencks. They are wildly unusual for Americans. For a while, Weldon sat on the Sand County Foundation Board with me. Kathy supplied the Nyangombi women with sewing machines, cloth, and thread to get their business off the ground. The thing she didn't supply was an actual business model that would allow the community to retail their work. Instead, Kathy buys everything (except that bunch of linen napkins Jackie bought) and stores it, as legend has it, in a warehouse in Charleston.

My dear wife, Jackie, a kind heart if there ever was one, after a few years of knowing Kathy Schenck, affectionately labeled her the "Wingnut."

Res Nullius

The story of private land conservancies in Zimbabwe is worth telling. The original ranches were put together from the late 1800s through the

1950s. They were large stretches of uninhabited Lowveld. When the land was cleared of wildlife and stocked with cattle, the colonists were in business. By 1975 it had become clear to the "farmers" that the cattle business was a bust. About the same time a couple of odd things happened. The government of Rhodesia declared that in the future, all game would be owned by the state; that is, the king owns the wildlife. Citizens who were in the wildlife business sued all the way to the Rhodesian Supreme Court. The court ruled against the government, and the Parks and Wildlife Act of 1975 made wildlife the property of no one (*res nullius*, in fact, "not owned by the king," or anyone else for that matter).

Any landowner or communal stakeholder controlling the location of game (like with a fence) could capitalize from the wildlife living on their land. The government developed scientific quota systems for hunting and monitoring of populations. The basics of the law is that if, for instance, you shot a hippo destroying your garden and he wandered off and died on your neighbor's lawn, your neighbor would own the meat. The Parks and Wildlife Act of 1975 was intended to create a business for native communities on communal lands alongside the national parks so that wildlife would be of value—value, that is, beyond poaching—by allowing for the creation of game management areas on communal/tribal lands. It inadvertently opened the door for the development of game preserves and conservancies on private properties.

At the same time, while some national park wildlife populations were being decimated by poaching, others were becoming severely overpopulated with big game. Remember the killing of whole herds of elephants? Elephants cannot be killed randomly or one at a time, like lions or Cape buffalo. Elephants do not forget being hunted. Not only that, there is strong evidence that they communicate with other herds by low frequency sound over long distances. An elephant five miles away from a killing might just take the offence out on you and stomp you to death. So, wildlife biologists came up with an answer: Cull entire herds, from the matriarch to the youngest babies.

Many biologists and environmentalists objected. Can you imagine? Biologists having to kill elephants to control overpopulation? Clem Coetsee and Clive Stockil came up with a plan to transport entire breeding herds of elephants to other areas—effectively restocking elephants on parts of the range where they had been previously killed off. Their theory followed a lesson learned from culling: If you kill the matriarch the herd will not leave her. What if you darted the matriarch? Would the entire herd stand around, trying to rouse her, long enough to dart the entire herd? They asked Parks to allow them to try.

The Zimbabwean National Parks agreed to try out the Clem & Clive plan. In 1993, some twenty-three herds from Gonarezhou National Park, a total of 534 animals, were darted and transported to the newly formed Save Valley Conservancy. Not a single elephant died. I wish I had been there. It must be the largest operation ever conducted in a national park. Think of all those giant trucks, cranes, game scouts, and veterinarians, as well as professional hunters armed with dart guns instead of bazookas. And me? I'd have found a way to volunteer.

Save Valley

Let me tell you about Save Valley Conservancy.

The geology and landforms of the Save Valley comprise a large part of the northernmost southeast Lowveld. The Lowveld sits below an escarpment at an elevation of about eight hundred feet above sea level at the Save River to around 2,500 feet elevation where it meets the escarpment. Most of Save Valley is around 1,300 feet. It is an old and worn out continental landmass. Erosion has worn very deep into the Earth's crust, exposing the billion-year-old Precambrian basement rock, which around there is mostly granite. The countryside is pretty flat. What might otherwise be endless and boring mopane forest and grassland savanna is punctuated here and there by differential weathering of the granite. The old weathered granite forms big and little boulders and exfoliation domes. Some balance precariously, one on top of another, creating a wonderland that looks like pebbles piled up by giants, or an Andy Goldsworthy installation. The little bouldery hills are called *kopjes*, Boer Dutch for "hill." (In general, Boer names totally lack imagination.)

A variety of endemic plants, shrubs, and succulents grow on the kopjes. Snakes love the kopjes. Leopards love the kopjes. Geologists love the kopjes. Wait a second, who cares about geologists when there are klipspringers? Klipspringers love the kopjes, too.

Klipspringers are little antelope about the size of a border collie. They have large, sad brown eyes topped with long, long lashes. They dance over the rocks on the tips of their little black hooves, which are cloven (they are even-toed ungulates) and pointed, just like a ballerina in toe shoes. Klipspringers mate for life. You always see them in pairs. If you see a single klipspringer, it's a widow(er).

The kopjes are also home to dassies, or rock hyrax. They're cute little buggers that chirp at you if you get too close. Their genealogy is weird: While they look like rodents, their nearest relatives are elephants!

Many of the granite kopjes form half domes hundreds, even a thousand feet tall. Some you can walk over and barely know they are there, except for the hard, black surface under your feet. All of them are "exfoliation domes." The granite, as it rose into the Earth's crust and cooled, developed radial, nearly but not quite horizontal lines of weakness. Once exposed to heating and cooling at the surface, the granite spalls off in thin sheets that follow a large arc. Anyhow, they are very picturesque little hills that dot the Lowveld.

This area of the southeast Lowveld was uninhabitable thorn-bush country. In a colonial map from the 1920s included in Alexandra Fuller's wonderful bestseller, *Don't Let's Go to the Dogs Tonight*, this area is described as "not fit for white man's habitation" (Random House, 2003). It was not fit for any human, in fact, white or black. It is desert, unfit for farming. Most of what is now the Save Valley Conservancy was acquired in the 1950s by the Devuli Ranch, on which Alexandra Fuller's family lived in the 1970s. Over time the Devuli Ranch, originally 750,000 acres, was subdivided into thirty-thousand- and sixty-thousand-acre parcels. Clive Stockil's parents managed one of those ranches. Eventually, Clive purchased two of the subdivided ranches: Senuko 1 and Senuko 2, sixty thousand acres of land in total.

The cattle farmers who purchased tracts of the Devuli Ranch finally came together in the late eighties and early nineties and decided to go into the wildlife business. They had concluded that cattle ranching was not sustainable after a series of catastrophic droughts. There were twenty-four farms, totaling 960,000 acres. They sold off their cattle; took down all the internal fencing; put up a double fourteen-foot-high electrified game fence; bought Cape buffalo, eland, kudu, zebra, and other game at auction; brought in elephants from Gonarezhou; and volunteered to take care of twenty of the one hundred black rhinos remaining in Zimbabwe. That's right, they were given the black rhinos by Zim National Parks Department on the terms that they would protect them, breed them, but not hunt them.

There are now more than 120 black rhinos at Save. They form the core of a trophy hunting and/or photo safari business that includes the "big five": Cape buffalo, rhino, elephant, lion, and leopard. The lion and leopard returned to Save on their own. Why not, there is a lot of (big) cat food there. Some of you may be scandalized by my mentioning trophy hunting and conservation in the same breath. Don't be. I'm no hunter, but I'm no Bambi Environmentalist either. Save Valley Conservancy is incredibly successful in terms of reintroduction of wildlife and increased biodiversity on a very large portion of the Lowveld ecosystem. Without the income to both expand the animal populations and, more importantly, protect the animals from poachers, their success would not have been possible.

For example, the African painted dog is considered by wildlife biologists to be the most endangered large predator in Africa. It is estimated that only three thousand remain. They also snuck into Save Valley on their own. They are not trophy animals, nor do they have much economic value. Instead, they eat potential trophy animals. Why then, do the conservancy partners protect them? Because they are conservationists first and business-men second. You wouldn't live out in this wild semidesert unless you loved the land and animals more than making a living. During a visit in 2005, I met two wild dog researchers studying the 213 wild dogs within the con-servancy, financed by a grant from the New England Zoo.

One other minor point: economic studies concluded that the farm-ers of the Zimbabwean Lowveld made, on average, 50¢ per acre per year on cattle, $4 on trophy hunting, and $10 on the photo safari business. Wildlife can pay for itself!

The private land conservancies are one of the great conservation sto-ries around. Too bad they have been threatened by the racist, despotic Mugabe government of Zimbabwe.

So, there I was visiting Hammond Ranch to interview the various conservation stakeholders. After a wonderful dinner, Russell and I were invited to visit Senuko Ranch, where Clive Stockil, the conservancy chairman, lives. Clive is famous for a number of things, but to me the most impressive is his hat. I thought I wore a pretty nasty, old, field hat—mine is a Stetson—which has seen such abuse as to inspire people to take my picture. But Clive's straw cowboy hat is even nastier. I'm not sure he even took it off to go to bed. I found out later that he buys about a dozen at a time. They don't last long out on the Lowveld.

The next evening, we showed up at Senuko Ranch for dinner with Lin, Clive's partner and a wildlife artist, among others. On an easel was a painting of wild dogs done by Lin. Being a Yank, I didn't wait very long to ask Lin if I could buy the painting.

"Lin, can I buy that painting, please?"

Lin laughed. "Wow, Ed, I'd love to sell it to you, but the oils are still wet. I just finished it this afternoon."

"Okay. Here's my schedule. If you can get it to Harare before I leave, I'll take it with me." The painting didn't cooperate, but Lin, a world-renowned wildlife artist, was scheduled to show her stuff at a safari convention in North Carolina a few months later. We invited her to visit and stay with us in Denver, which she did. She also brought along my painting in the process.

Clive got on the shortwave radio and called his neighbor, Willie Papst. I was invited to dinner the following evening at Pabst's place, Sanga, about fifty kilometers north of Hammond. Weldon volunteered to drive Russell and me up there. Willie, a German industrialist billionaire, owns about 120,000 acres inside Save.

With Weldon behind the wheel and me on the left-hand front passenger side (it's British right-side drive, of course) we took off for Willie's just before dusk. August is early winter in the Southern hemisphere. The weather was balmy. I was sitting with my elbow out the open window when, all of a sudden, Weldon swerved to the right. Then swerved back to the left. Then slid to a halt. My heart was in my throat. I thought we were going to roll. Weldon and Russell were shouting.

What the hell are they shouting? Oh! They're yelling at me.

"Did you see it? Did you see it?"

"See what?" I asked in a perfectly calm voice. You don't believe me? Okay. "See what?" I squeaked, choking on dust and terror.

"The bull eland by the side of the road," replied Weldon.

"Its head was over the bonnet!" Russell blurted out at the same time.

"Oh yeah, that brown and white-striped wall," I muttered.

I turned around to look at Russell. I'd never seen his normally pink face the color of chalk.

Russell explained, "Ed, eland jump when they're scared. They kill more people in cars than any other animal. This bull saw us and, I swear, pulled his head back just as Weldon swerved. Another two seconds and you would have lost your arm. Any other eland and he would have joined us in the cab. We were dead, man, only we aren't."

A bull eland is the largest antelope in the world. They weigh in around 1,300 pounds.

Whew! Sounds ridiculous, but a month later Deb Gundlach, a friend who lives in Harare, had a greater kudu jump in her cab. She spent six weeks in the hospital having her bones wired back together. A kudu is less than one-third the size of an eland.

I won't say much about dinner at Willie's place except that the safari lodge was over the top. The incredible main building was a high ceiling, thatched roof, open-air structure supported by immense leadwood logs. It was impressive.

"Where'd you get leadwood trees that size?" I asked Willie.

"Remember those trees I showed you along the banks of the Runde?" chimed in Russell.

"Oh yeah," I said, "the ones the Parks Department girdled and killed to prevent tsetse fly epidemics."

Rhodesian health officials had decided that tsetse flies wouldn't fly inland if there were no large trees along the riverbanks. Don't ask me where they came up with that conclusion. Guess what? They were wrong. They killed thousands of five-hundred-year-old leadwood trees for nothing. Since leadwood trees are known to remain standing for up to a thousand years after they die, there are still plenty around to harvest for building.

The trouble with leadwood is that it is virtually impossible to work. It's aptly named. Just cutting a leadwood tree down is an all-day affair—it's the toughest, heaviest wood imaginable. It won't even float in water. Willie had been amused at the idea of using leadwood in cabinetry. He took Weldon, Russell, and me to his master suite. A humongous leadwood log formed the support along one corner of the room. Willie put a key into an almost invisible five-foot-tall "doorway" and opened it. We were looking into a gun cabinet.

"My cabinetmaker refused to make ze gun closet," he said. "I let him know zatt he would do any cabinet vork I asked of him." Need I remind you? Willie is a billionaire, after all.

As we walked back out into the main hall, Russell bent over and whispered, "Lotta good that'll do him when the place burns down!"

CHAPTER 9

The 18-Karat Rolex

THE NEXT MORNING RUSSELL AND I were back down at Senuko Ranch. Clive had promised me a look at a black rhino. Remember, white rhinos are big, fat, social lawnmowers. Black rhinos are browsers. They live in thorn-bush country, are nearly blind, have ears like radar dishes, and can smell almost as well as they can hear. They will charge anything that makes them nervous. Considering that they are certifiably insane, you gotta assume anything you do will make them nervous.

The first rule of black rhino tracking is to have a climbable tree handy at all times. It's great advice. Trouble is, acacia thorn-bush country harbors few climbable trees.

We drove off in the Land Cruiser, "Alpha One," staying in contact with Jackson and his scouts by shortwave radio. Clive stopped the vehicle. Not one hundred meters ahead, a herd of Cape buffalo were crossing the road. Yellow-billed oxpeckers flitted across their backs, picking parasites out of their ears and off their skin. I once read a paper on oxpecker eating habits. The conventional wisdom had been that oxpeckers eat parasites, a truly symbiotic relationship with the Cape buffalo. Ornithologists discovered that the stomach contents of oxpeckers contained on average 40 percent blood. They should be named "yellow-billed bloodsuckers!" (The stomach contents of cleaner wrasses, those little blue and yellow tropi-cal fish, are the same—a neat example of convergent evolution—well at least, shared eating habits of wildly different critters.)

The buffalo herd moved off, but not until at least five hundred had crossed the dirt track. "How many buffalo do you have on Save Valley?" I asked.

"By last year's game count, about five thousand," replied Clive. "It's really hard to get an accurate count of buffalo. A ranch manager can count three hundred one day, and the herd could move fifteen kilometers overnight and be counted by another ranch manager the next day. That's why we combine road counts with an annual fly-over survey."

We came to a patch of sand veldt. You can tell by the change in the soil color and the foliage. Big umbrella acacias like the sand, as do perennial grasses. We stopped for a while and waited. A couple of hundred meters north, a herd of about twenty-five doe impala with their dominant buck were grazing on grass. To the east, a herd of wildebeest, maybe a hundred or so, stirred nervously. A call came over the radio. Clive started the Land Cruiser and took off.

The first rhino spotted by the game scouts that morning was a mother with a two-week-old baby. We climbed down from the truck and started walking. *Why didn't we go looking for another rhino*, I wondered all morn-ing. *Couldn't we track a nice, safe, full-grown bull instead?*

Three trackers were spread out ahead of us. Clive was in front of me, and Russell behind. Nonetheless, I did not feel safe. Mostly, I felt like I must have been out of my mind to agree to try this. The rhino mom kept retreating in front of us, leading us into thicker and thicker thorn bush.

All of a sudden the three trackers were running straight toward me. The rhino was charging! Clive turned, his eyes as big as saucers, and began to run straight at me. I didn't have time to think. I spun around and ran like a bat out of hell. Thirty seconds later, I looked around (from my perch in a dead tree of some kind), and realized I was out in front of the whole group. Russell walked over.

"How'd you do that, mate? I started in the lead and you ended up ahead of me. Jesus, Ed, you're twenty years older than me!"

"You know what they say, Russell."

"What do they say, Ed?" Russell said with that "I know what's coming" look on his face.

"When the bear is chasing you, you don't have to be the fastest. You only have to be faster than the next fastest."

"But, Ed, you were the fastest."

"Russell, I couldn't see anyone else, all I could see was your back. I didn't find that at all satisfactory."

Russell and I found a big old pod mahogany tree to sit under. Clive wandered off to check up on the rhino and baby. I couldn't sit still—I was more than a bit amped up after our narrow escape from death by the pissed-off mother rhino. So I wandered around the tree, kicking up debris with the toe of my Teva. I wanted to find the seed of the pod mahogany. The pods are pretty nondescript, but the seeds inside are almost ebony black, tipped with vivid yellowish-orange, and look for all the world like an acorn on psychedelic drugs.

"Ed, do you know how hard it is to find a pod mahogany seed? All the animals love them. Especially baboons."

I wasn't deterred and after about fifteen minutes, I turned one up. I tried to hand it off to Russell, but he refused to take it.

"You never give away a pod mahogany seed. It's called the 'good luck seed.' Hang on to it."

He looked me up and down. "I reckon you're going to need a passel of good luck if you keep working in Zimbabwe."

An hour later, Clive joined us under the tree.

"All's well with mum and baby," he said. "That wasn't a really close call, you know. It's when you're in the open and they have a bead on you that you're in big trouble."

I could sense a story coming: Clive is a terrific storyteller. "Sounds like you've been in one of those jams already, huh, Clive?"

"Didn't you see me on CBS in '94 when they did the piece on rhino poaching?"

"Musta missed it. Tell us about it."

"Well, they sent a film crew with a New York producer here to Senuko. We had just got the rhinos a coupla years before, so they weren't as comfortable with the place as they are now."

That was a "comfortable" rhino that had just chased us, I thought.

"We were tracking a big bull through moderately open savanna, when he turned around and stepped out from behind a bush—right out in the open.

"The cameraman was right behind me, resting his camera on my left shoulder. The producer (he named him—a famous guy) was about ten meters behind us with a 35 mm camera in his hand. The rhino was looking straight at us from a distance of only thirty meters. I turned a little to whisper to both of them, 'Don't move!'

"The wind was okay, but at that distance any movement could provoke the rhino into a charge. It was a Mexican standoff."

Where'd he get that phrase?

"We must have stood there for ten minutes. The camera continued to run the whole time—*whirr, whirr.* The rhino could obviously hear it, but it was like background noise—a little annoying, maybe, but not enough to convince him to go crazy.

"About that moment, the New York producer stepped out from behind me and took a picture with his camera. 'Click.' The rhino charged right at him."

Serves him right, I thought. *Trample the dummy, Mr. Rhino.*

Clive paused for a second. I could see that telling this story, even after all these years, still moved him.

"I did the only thing I could think of. As the rhino charged past me, I hit him at the shoulder, with a rugby tackle. That great big head turned with amazing grace, hooked me, and flipped me through the air. Later we measured the distance of the toss at twenty-five meters. I landed pretty hard. Had a broken hip and ankle, though the ankle may have occurred when the rhino stepped on me."

"The rhino stepped on you?" I blurted.

"Yeah, after he threw me, he turned in his tracks and came right after me. As he ran me over, he put his head down to gore me. Took all the buttons off my shirt without breaking the skin. I think my ankle went at that moment, but I really can't be sure."

"It's some kind of miracle he didn't open you up like a tin can," I said, considering the three-foot-long horns I've seen on big black rhino bulls.

"Well, ya see, Ed, I'm a lucky bloke. All the rhinos had had their horns sawed off for transport in '92. In two year's time, this bugger's horn was only about a foot long and still blunt on the working end. I think he kinda misjudged the distance to my belly."

We all laughed.

Ho, ho, I thought, *Clive's belly must have been a lot smaller in '94.*

So Clive counts himself among the "lucky." If you saw where he lives, doing what he loves, you'd count him among the lucky, too.

After a pause, Clive continued, "Several months after the incident, a package arrived at Senuko all the way from New York. In it was an 18-karat gold Rolex watch. Inscribed on the inside are the sincere thanks of the CBS producer."

I've never seen Clive without the watch on his wrist. (A more detailed and slightly different form of this story was published in Keith Meadows' *Sometimes When It Rains.*)

Who is this Clive Stockil guy, anyway? Clive's parents ran a cattle ranch on what is now Save Valley Conservancy. Clive grew up playing in the bush with Shangaan kids from the Mahenya community. Shangaans are a subgroup of the Zulu nation, who abandoned Shaka Zulu after invading and defeating the Tsonga nation in the 1830s. The Shangaans stayed north of the Limpopo River to avoid being hunted down and massacred by a very annoyed Shaka Zulu. After years, some snuck back into Zululand and gathered up their wives. Naturally, the

Europeans managed to place a national border right through the middle of their homeland.

In addition to learning English, Clive learned to speak Shangaan and Shona, the two major African languages of Rhodesia. When Clive was ten years old, at boarding school, he sleepwalked in the middle of the night and pitched right through a second story window. He drove his right hand and forearm straight into the turf. The nearest doctor, Colin Saunders, in Chiredzi, worked for days to save his arm. The arm is marginally functional at best. Clive does everything, including shooting, from the left. He's of medium height and built like a tree stump. He will outwalk anyone, carrying a .458 caliber elephant gun all day. More than that, he's a university-educated conservationist, an amazing birder, and possibly the best tracker in Southern Africa.

Clive is the heart and soul behind the formation of the Save Valley Conservancy. Working with international wildlife organizations like the Beit Trust, WWF, IUCN, and International Rhino Foundation (IRF), Clive, with the support of folks like Raoul du Toit, made SVC possible. He was the chairman of the conservancy for its first nineteen years. In 2013, Clive was awarded the Tusk Conservation Award by Prince William, the future king of England.

—

I returned home from this trip with the promise of an oil painting depicting a pack of wild dogs done by Lin Barrie, a near certainty that I would be Clive Stockil's partner in Senuko Ranch, and the makings of a relationship between the Save Valley Conservancy and Sand County Foundation, with the latter serving as a science liaison for the Save Valley Conservancy. I don't mean to brag, but early on, I knew that Clive would need financial support to keep Senuko Ranch. I could foresee the domino effect that might occur if the Save Valley Conservancy, the greatest experiment in private lands conservation, fell apart. We were at a tipping point in history and I could intervene. So, down the road, I did.

CHAPTER 10

On the Road in Namibia

WE ARRIVED IN WINDHOEK, THE capital of Namibia, on June 10 and immediately set off to find our vehicles. The car agency is owned by a couple of Boers who are mildly obnoxious—that's not a terribly unusual condition for these folks. Not only did they announce that we can't tow our camp trailer on their vehicles, their vehicles were not adequate for the ten passengers and supplies necessary for our field trek. After a half hour of dickering we swapped a Mazda for a big Land Cruiser, but not until I had put $105,000 Namibian ($18,000 US) on my credit cards as insurance. I was sure they were going to rape us on road dings to the paint job, but c'est la vie.

Our first day of meetings was terrific. Various NGOs and the Ministry of Environment and Tourism (MET), the government agency in charge of tourism, filled us in on the legislation and history of conservancy establishment in northwestern Namibia. The only fly in the ointment appeared Saturday night when the school next door to our guesthouse held some kind of big bash, celebrating some sporting event like roller hockey or some such thing. The band began playing at about 7 p.m. and didn't quit 'til midnight. I put in my South African Airways earplugs but I could still hear, or more accurately, feel the bass from the band. By

11 p.m. I was contemplating the Windhoek *Times Examiner*'s headline for Sunday: "Maniacal Tourist Murders Band Member at Local School." I finally fell asleep.

Fred Nelson and I got a late start out of Windhoek next morning. Fred, our man in Arusha, ran SCF's community-based conservation work with the Maasai. One of his leaders, Mary, had an expired passport, so she spent the morning trying to get temporary papers in Nairobi. The contingency plan was for her to arrive at 2 p.m. the day of our departure to the bush, so one vehicle would stay behind to meet her. Since the first day's drive was eight hours, and driving in the bush after dark is not particularly safe, this would be a real setback. Thanks to the world of mobile phones, Fred got word by 10:30 a.m. that Mary's temporary papers were rejected at the Tanzanian border, so she wouldn't be joining us after all. In hindsight, it was a lucky break. We really didn't have enough room in the vehicles for another body.

We met up in Ohondjombo at 11:30 a.m. and were on our way. The tar road on the first 450 kilometers of our journey was great: We saw greater kudu, dik-dik, and giraffe. Traveling the gravel stretch of road after dark, with the cows coming home, was somewhat more exciting. About four kilometers from Outjo, our night's destination, the Mazda busted a tire on a rock. The Mazda was supposed to have two spares. It only had one, and it was flat.

Those damn Boers are going to get an earful when we get back, I thought.

It only took an hour and a half to find a manual tire pump in Outjo. Four of us traded off pumping up the tire and then we set off to find beer and dinner. God, did that beer taste good. We also enjoyed some strange tasting chicken and really good ribs. The Maasai ate T-bone steaks. They have rather expensive taste in food—at least when somebody else is paying.

Our guesthouse accommodations were basic. The hot water pipes were plugged with lime, or so I found out when I stepped into the freezing shower. Aino, our guide, and Liz, who works with Fred, were in the girl's side of the head when I stepped under the shower. I'm sure they got a laugh from hearing me scream, "Shit! Shit! Shit!" as I bathed in the cold water. Aino Pavo, by the way, of the Owambo tribe from near the Angolan border of Namibia, has a Finnish name. Nineteenth century Finnish missionaries, of all things, gave all her village members Finnish names. Typical mzungus!

Me and my friend Aino Pavo on a hill in the Namib Desert.

I really enjoyed traveling with our group. Our team of brave trekkers included four Maasai: Christopher Kissyoki Ole Memantoki with Sand County Foundation; Peter Sailenyi Ole Ndoipo from Ewor Endeke, near Longido; Christopher Ole Nduruai, chairman of Engare Sero village near Lake Natron; and Kibiriti Ole Tipap, chairman of Loiborsirret village near Tarangire National Park. Fred Nelson, director of our West Kilimanjaro project, Liz Singleton, his new sidekick, Mike Jones SCF's

Africa Community Based Conservation Network director, Aino, and me rounded out the team.

Our travel problems continued the next morning. The flat wasn't just flat, it was busted, so we had no spare for the Mazda. Christopher M., who was also our mechanic, was not pleased. No field vehicle should operate on tubeless tires! It was Sunday and we couldn't possibly find a tube. With no town for nearly four days travel, we were in the hands of fate.

I didn't sleep well because Mike kept me awake with his snoring. I stayed pretty chipper but I had to figure out how to catch some Zs. Since I love being in the bush, I decided to sleep out on the ground for the next nine nights—unless there are lions or hyenas around. If I stare at the stars long enough I fall asleep.

—

This whole field trip was planned pretty much without me. In April 2004, just as Jackie and I were about to move into our new house, and after enduring twenty-two months of drawings, construction, and almost no travel to Africa, Mike asked me to join him on a field conference in Namibia as the American representative of SCF. My role with SCF is to review existing projects, evaluate potential new projects, and attend conferences. Mike had kindly refrained from dangling trips in front of me because he knew about the house project and is a good friend to my wife.

Jackie gave me one of those ghastly looks when I mentioned the Namibia field trip about twenty-two seconds after I got off the phone. Yes, I took three deep breaths before I spoke to her.

"You want to leave our new house right after we have moved in?"

I recognized this was not actually a question. It was a challenge. "Well . . ." I petered out before I could say any more.

Two days later, Jackie looked across the dinner table and said, "This is one of those 'once in a lifetime things,' isn't it?" Before I could open my mouth, she added, "You'll really hate yourself if you don't go?" So, I got the go-ahead without even having to make the case for traveling nine thousand miles to sleep on the ground. What a woman!

The objective of this trip was to bring together the Maasai from southern Kenya and northern Tanzania, the Himba, a seminomadic pastoralist tribe, the Heraro, mostly sedentary "farmers," and the Cape Coloured. The Cape Coloured group is descended from San Bushman and Hottentot tribes crossed with Boers during the colonial period—the period when the Hottentots and San Bushmen were virtual slaves.

The idea of native community management of conservancies, cooked up by the Namibian Parliament, promotes tourism, and gives the authority to make business deals directly to the indigenous people living on communal land. The income thus stays in the villages. Those of you that think that a nomadic cattle herder might be out of place in a conference on community-based conservation are misinformed.

Our first day in Windhoek was filled with lectures from the various Namibian NGOs and government agencies. I sat in the back during the first two talks, wondering how, with all my various plug converters, I didn't have the variety needed in Namibia.

The Maasai, on the other hand, sat attentively at the conference table scribbling away frantically. They took more and better notes than a college student attending a lecture by his favorite professor. They also asked the most penetrating questions.

For example, "What good is wildlife if you don't get land ownership?"

The Maasai are mostly literate, very interested in making money, educating their children, and somehow preserving their culture. They are also not shy. One day, during our drive, Christopher asked Aino whether the Namibian tribes practice male and female circumcision. Her response started a half-hour discussion about the practice and criticism of Western abhorrence of female circumcision. I managed to keep my big mouth shut.

Marienfluss

After eight hours of driving, we finally arrived in Marienfluss. We drove over some of the nastiest "road" I've ever been on: upturned slates and schists of the Precambrian complex. One section that looked like a steep, narrow wash covered with knife-edge outcroppings of golden, micaceous schist really threw a wrench in our progress. In order to make it across, all the passengers jumped out and walked alongside the vehicles to guide the drivers so they didn't bust any more tires.

Yes, folks, that's what they call a "road" in Marienfluss, Namibia.

The countryside is quite spectacular. Sere mountainsides of schist, gneiss, mylonitized granite, and granite gneiss. The schist is shiny gray, but, due to the micas being altered to chlorite, glows golden in the light of the rising and setting sun. The landscape is dotted with small, rounded hillsides of black mica schist on which nothing grows. Endemic euphorbias, a couple of candelabra types and one that has many sticklike green stems, dot other hillsides. The latter variety is so poisonous that it has killed people who put dead branches on their fire, just from inhaling the smoke. There is also a plant, commonly called "elephant's foot," that is unbelievable unless you actually see it. Imagine an elephant's leg cut off about a foot off the ground, with two or three little twigs branching out of the top. It typically bears no leaves, leafing out only after a rain. Rain occurs once every five or ten years in this area, so it's not a common sight.

Just around dark, driving through the Hartmannsberg Valley we saw two gemsbok, the first at a couple of hundred yards, the second right alongside the Land Cruiser. They are possibly the most beautiful antelopes on earth. As we approached the Kunene River we were surprised by the appearance of one very drunk Himba fellow who ran out of the dark and jumped onto the vehicle. He was very insistent that Mike follow his directions to find our campsite. I wondered if we were being led into the bushes to an ambush. Fortunately we popped out of the reeds into the back end of our campsite. By 8:30 the tents were pitched and we had meat cooking on the fire. We had sundowners (drinks at sundown, of course) on the bank of the Kunene River, looking toward Angola. We hit the hay around ten. As soon as I lay down on the ground, I saw four meteors, two nearly in tandem together, streak across the sky.

The Himba people live in the northwestern corner of Namibia, from the Atlantic Ocean to the mopane scrubland roughly five hundred kilometers east. It is the most remote desert area I have ever visited. Beyond the Namib, one of the most inhospitable and probably oldest deserts in the world (20 mm average rainfall annually), rows of low hills, composed of very ancient and worn down Precambrian terrain, are covered, if you can call it that, with scant vegetation.

Marienfluss is the northwesternmost conservancy in Namibia. It's two days very hard drive from Windhoek, more than eight hours north of Opuwo, a little Heraro town that has nothing to offer. The area will never be famous for its wildlife, unless a traveler is somehow really interested in the very specific species. Only four species of large mammals are native to the area: springbok, gemsbok or oryx, giraffe, and the rare Hartmann's mountain zebra. Wilderness Safari has an upscale camp on the Kunene River within the conservancy (awarded years ago by the colonial government) that advertises that there are no game drives! There's just sand and river, and more sand and river. For this, visitors can pay $600 per night per couple. What they can do is visit with the Himba, one of the most exotic-looking people on earth.

Our campsite ran about $6 per campsite, sleeping as many people as you can pack in. There are six sites and I have it on good authority, that in season as many as twenty vehicles can be found at the campground. It doesn't seem possible that anyone would drive this far for a holiday in one of the hottest deserts imaginable, but I know a little of the South African: they will drive to hell and back for a bargain.

I was there in the middle of winter and the temperature must have topped out at close to 90 degrees Fahrenheit. I brought all kinds of cold weather gear for camping out in the desert and, even though we are just off the river, I had to kick off my socks and baseball pants in order to cool off. I also shed the blanket from atop my lightweight sleeping bag. Even overheated, sleeping on sand is very comfortable.

During our only full-day stop, the Maasai and Himba conducted a meeting under a big acacia tree. Lucky, a Himba chief and Integrated Rural Development and Nature Conservation (IRDNC) employee translated from English to Himba while Christopher Kissyoki Ole Memantoki translated from English to Ma. The introductions only lasted an hour, as the Maasai and Himba tried to keep their stories short. Christopher asked me to explain what I did, so I talked about SCF. But he really wanted me to explain what a geologist does.

When Christopher explained to the Himba, with his tongue in his cheek, that the Maasai were famous cattle thieves, the Himba women looked at him with such hostility that I started to imagine our throats being cut while we slept. Cattle are as important to the Himba as they are to the Maasai. However, the Maasai clans tend to pilfer cattle from other clans or, especially, from whites.

We were very concerned about Christopher sticking his foot in his mouth. He had inadvertently and seriously jeopardized our safety. He finally, being long-winded (a five-minute talk in Africa lasts at least a half hour), got around to convincing his audience that his comment was really a joke. It only took the Himba about ten minutes to get it. As the hostility left their faces, I began to relax.

The exchange of stories was really very interesting. While the Maasai are a Nilotic people and the Himba Bantu, their traditions have amazing parallels. Their cattle culture, marriage ceremony, singing, and mythology seem to be very similar. The primary difference seemed to me to be in their way of governance. The Maasai make decisions by consensus, not majority rule, which leads to a village support system for elected government. The Himba maintain a local chieftain system that leads to centralized decision making instead of democracy. The Himba proudly let us know that they were about to get their first school—a trailer-like conveyance dragged around the countryside servicing first through third graders.

After our morning session we bought a goat from the Himba—dinner with the Maasai was always meat, meat, and more meat. Believe it or not, I'd never seen an animal slaughtered in my fifty-eight years. The Himba butcher spent several minutes pressing on the goat's carotid artery before sticking a sharp knife into the artery. After about thirty seconds he slit the goat's throat, cutting all the way to the bone. It would be nice to report that the goat died peacefully but, in fact, it kicked and twitched for about ten minutes. I wasn't feeling so hot after watching the slaughter. But I'm a hardy soul and I recovered; I had no trouble eating my share of goat that evening.

After dinner, the Himba returned from their village. They had butchered the goat and left us to enjoy it. About five women, ten men, and a like number of kids from ages five through fifteen participated in singing and dancing. The Maasai song and dance is very melodic and rhythmic. The Himba sing a cappella and their dances consist of jumping up and down, stomping the ground, and flinging themselves about wildly. The night's dance ended in a near collision with a woman, apparently a social transgression.

They hung around for a while after their performance and asked the Maasai to dance some more. Unfortunately, they declined. See, they were village elders; Maasai dancing is normally done by young warriors. I think they were exhausted. After standing around some while longer the Himba asked for a lift back to their village. We all looked around at each other and not too politely declined. We thought better of leaving our camp and potentially finding ourselves in a less than safe situation. They looked somewhat shocked but shortly turned on their heels and walked off.

In the morning, we rose before dawn, packed up our camp, ate PB&J

on bread with tea or coffee, and headed off down the road. We were nervous about spending another eight hours on the road with no spare for the Mazda. Somehow we made it to Purros Conservancy campground in a mere five hours. Along the way we saw no fewer than fifteen, maybe even twenty, gemsbok, a dozen kori bustards, and Rüppell's korhaan, an endemic bird with a painfully skinny neck.

The Purros campground is beautiful. It's down in the riverbed with many large camel thorn trees shading the soft, sandy ground. While we were setting up camp a herd of desert elephants came down through the trees, working its way toward our camp. Fred, Aino, and I snuck up on them, snapping photos from no more than thirty meters distance.

I was worried they would hear or smell our presence. Testing the breeze with dust, I was shocked to discover we were crosswind, sometimes even upwind from the elephants. It was not a safe spot. I watched in alarm as a youngster sniffed us out and flapped his ears. Finally, the matriarch emerged from the trees to shoo us away. She was quite delicate about her request, simply lifting her right front foot and sniffing before she charged. We spun and hightailed it back to our campsite. The elephants stuck around, hanging out about one hundred meters from camp. We begrudged their presence, as they kept us from using the head.

In the morning I found elephant tracks. They were hard to miss, as the only very large, oval depressions in the land. The herd was still nearby, grazing roughly forty meters from our campsite. Fortunately, they never walked into our camp, seeing as how I preferred to sleep rough, out on the ground. Very civilized for elephants.

We spent a very nice morning lazing around, finally breaking camp around 9 a.m. The Purros Conservancy folks hadn't shown up the night before but, as this is Africa where being on time is pretty rare, we weren't surprised when they finally showed up at 9:57 a.m.—within three minutes of our departure. Mike had the engine running on the Land Cruiser, that's how close we were to leaving. Naturally, we changed our day's plans and drove over to their office and had a meeting.

Christopher gave the fastest introduction of nine people ever executed under the African sky. The conservancy people got the hint, making their introductions in only a half hour. For another hour and a half we discussed and mostly questioned the running of the Purros Conservancy. How much money do you make from the campground? Do you have joint ventures? How many people are employed? They shared with us that a joint venture with Sun Safaris will support the construction of an upmarket lodge by the river that will start with eight beds to be expanded to twelve as soon as occupancy can support the expansion. Sun Safaris has guaranteed the conservancy 5 percent of a minimum take of one million dollars. It's a nice start for the conservancy, which for the immediate future is entirely supported by the nonprofit IRDNC.

Sesfontein

We made a short drive through a narrow valley surrounded by brilliantly sparkling mountainsides of mica schist. The hillsides were dotted with the most amazing looking branching euphorbia trees, probably euphorbia virosa or "poisonous spurge." To this point in my travels I thought baobabs were the funniest-looking trees I'd ever see. But these trees reminded me of saguaro cactus, but smaller and thinner, with branches sticking out in a wilder and more random fashion. They are members of the Euphorbia family, endemic to the Namib and terribly poisonous if eaten or burned. Aino told us the unfortunate story of a family of campers that had died from using the plant as firewood. They inhaled the poison smoke. It seems as if nothing grows in the Namib that is benign. Either it will stick you or poison you.

We crossed a small set of hills, and the terrain and, naturally, the geology completely changed. Everything became soft and rounded, in shape and in color. The limestone or low-grade marble was gray, pink, and white intermixed with gray-brown shale. We had crossed an enormous fault zone with miles of vertical displacement. On one side we could see the lower part of the Earth's crust. On the other side, there were sediments that were a billion years younger.

We drove into Sesfontein, or Six Springs in the White Namib desert, at 4 p.m., after a mere four hours on the road, and found the tire shop. The sign outside listed "Michelin" and other European tire company names, but the shop had nothing more than a handmade metal ram to remove the tire from the rim and a bicycle pump. The mechanic fixed the tire in less than an hour and then went to work on the Land Cruiser's exhaust, which had fallen apart the day before. With a handmade gasket, wire, and bolts he reassembled it quite nicely. The total for tire and repair was about twelve bucks American.

The Sesfontein Conservancy folks weren't around so we stocked up on beer and pop and made our way to the campsite. I drank more beer—of the cold and warm varieties—on this trip than I usually drink in a year. That's not saying much since I don't really drink beer unless I'm eating Mexican food. But on this trip, a cold beer on a dusty trail tasted mighty fine.

Our campsite at Ongongo featured a warm spring for showering, thatched roofed lean-tos (we hardly used them) for shelter, and flush toilets (you know what those are for!). It was a poor conservancy with no upmarket tour operations or safari, but the campsite was nice.

The spring was fed by a little waterfall that dropped over an old tufa deposit onto river gravel. Vines crawled over the little cliff face and reeds lined the bank. It was quite a romantic little spot. The water was cool, but in a few spots warm spring water welled up from beneath the gravel bed. In the past there must have been much warmer and much more spring water—the surrounding countryside was littered and likely even underlain by tufa deposits, which is a variety of limestone formed by carbonate minerals from ambient temperature water bodies.

I slept out again, for the fourth night in a row. I was partly sheltered by a big mopane tree. As I lay on my back watching the night sky, a little caterpillar fell and landed on my face. *Was it a baby mopane worm*, I wondered as I rolled over and went to sleep. The next morning I noticed a rock under my pillow. It hadn't phased my hard head in the least.

Twyfelfontein and the Torra Conservancy

Our next stop was Twyfelfontein, or "twelve springs" in Afrikaans, famous for its bushman rock drawings. Along the way, the Land Cruiser busted a tire, our third on the trip. Our trip was only a couple of hundred kilometers, so we stopped several times.

Fred Nelson has the most amazing eyesight. He spotted five Hartmann's mountain zebra on a hillside. At first, all I could see was the cattle down below them. Further on we met with the Conservancy personnel at Torra. They are one of the oldest and most successful conservancies in Namibia, founded in 1998. They stopped accepting support from IRDNC in 2000, have a well padded savings fund, distribute dividends of about US $110 per year to their members, and maintain several joint ventures with high-end tour operators, including Wilderness Safaris.

In 2001, the members voted out their entire committee and hired an international accounting firm to manage their business. They have three more joint ventures in the works and have issued concessions to tour operators, while restricting land use to wildlife business (i.e., no livestock or settlements). It's a great use of their 810,000 acres by the eight hundred members of the conservancy. The conservancy chairman proudly informed us that based on financial projections the members could expect to receive close to $1,000 per year when the new concessions are fully operational. It may not sound like much to an American, but the average rural African can expect to earn somewhere between $40 and $400 per year.

—

I've been fascinated by the San Bushmen ever since my first trip to Africa as a tourist. At the first camp we visited in Botswana, Wilderness Safari's

Chitabe, my guide, Newman, was a San Bushman. He was a small fellow with yellowish skin, a perfectly round head, and hair buzzed very short. He had been brought up in the Kalahari and taught to track by his grandfather. Newman had also sought a formal Western education and become qualified as a safari guide.

I persuaded him to guide me on solo walks through the bush during my days at Chitabe. "Newman," I asked him, "please explain exactly what you see when you track and how you do it. Also, could you give me the name of every plant and animal in English, Latin, and San?"

At one point, we were walking along when a bull elephant sauntered between us and a tree-filled "island" rising above the grassy plain. Suddenly the elephant squawked and ran off. We had the wind and he was about 150 meters away. I had no idea what spooked him.

"Newman," I said, "how did he know we were there?"

"Eddie, look at the kudu, next to the trees." Newman was looking just beyond where the elephant had crossed.

I searched the island with my binoculars. "They're staring at us, aren't they?"

"The elephant didn't know what was nearby, but as soon as he saw the kudu's alarm, he took off." It's amazing what you see when you learn how to look.

Sitting with the Torra Conservancy committee, I covertly watched and admired the Cape Coloured. I remind you that following World War I, South Africa was given German Southwest Africa as a protectorate. The Boers, a notoriously hypocritical and highly religious group, had fathered many mixed-race children while governing. So, they took the opportunity to round up all their mixed-race offspring and ship them into the desert where they were expected to perish. They didn't. They were handed broken eggs and they made a hell of an omelet out of it. Of all the native peoples of Namibia, the Cape Coloured are the most highly educated, have the best business acumen, and, at least from the little I saw, are the most sanguine and contented.

After leaving the meeting we hooked a right and drove about ten kilometers toward the coast because I wanted to see one of the most bizarre plants in the world: Welwitschia. Welwitschia, endemic to Namibia, looks more than half dead and is all of two leaves growing on either side of a central corm. The leaves split and resplit over time, making it look generally pathetic. Oh boy! They had to drag me back to the Land Cruiser.

Welwitschia only grows on highly weathered basalt lava flows that underlie and are now found between the red sand dunes of the Namib Desert. It never rains in this area, about forty miles inland, but fog blows inland off the Skeleton Coast's cold ocean current. Welwitschia's leaves are perfectly arranged to collect any condensation that dribbles down into the center of the plant.

I looked it up: 27 percent of the plants found in Namibia are endemic species, meaning not found anywhere else. If you combine those of the Kalahari and Namib, the number is 51 percent.

We camped in a high-end campground. Our campsite is only twenty-five meters from the bathrooms and the bar. Cold beer and maybe a whiskey tonight!

We took off at 4:30 p.m. to visit the bushman rock art. The drawings are scraped out of desert varnish (manganese oxide) with crude quartz tools. The animal drawings are wonderfully accurate. Our biologist argued with our guide as to whether the rhinos were white or black. I'm not sure how they couldn't see the difference in the shape of the mouths and curve of the horns. We could also recognize kudu, giraffe, zebra, ostrich, springbok, and other fauna. Even the tiny Rüppell's korhaan was clearly identifiable. The rocks are coarse red fluvial sandstones interbedded with thin conglomerate layers; my guess is that they are in the Karoo geological formation of the Permian age.

Back in camp the mzungus sat around drinking beer. The Maasai drank Coca-Cola. Mike, while walking back from the bar with a cold beer (*Hey! Where's mine?*), found bull elephant spore about ten feet from where I was sitting by the fire. The spore crossed our Mazda track, meaning the elephant must have come through sometime between 4:30 and 6 p.m.

I wrote for a while, hit the head, dropped by the bar for another four cold beers, and promptly got lost on the hundred-meter walk back to camp in the dark. Mike claims it's because my brain is wired for the Northern hemisphere, so I turn the wrong way wherever I go in the Southern hemisphere. Who am I to argue?

—

We headed to the coast the next morning. Several of the Maasai who were traveling with us had never seen the ocean! Our drive was more than 650 kilometers, but the last three hundred were on tar road. On the way we passed a steenbok and a cheetah. Can you imagine? A cheetah crossing a road!

Namibia has the largest population, on private and communal lands, of three animals—the black rhino, the cheetah, and the Hartmann's mountain zebra. Thus, this empty and barren sere desert, with its wide-open spaces and small human populations, is a very poor, but very important habitat. Tying it all together are the new communal land conservancies that we visited. Before they are done, the Namibians will have conserved over thirty million semicontiguous acres. There is no fencing between the conservancies, either. They recognize that in any given year, a herd of springbok might find water and grass anywhere over a two-hundred-mile range.

We asked about the black rhino population and got a funny, if not perfectly reasonable answer: "We don't tell the public how many black rhinos are out here."

Considering the poaching of black rhinos in the 1980s, the less that is reported on rhino populations the better. The field officers did report to us that the population is growing. Our educated guess is that there must be in excess of three hundred rhinos roaming around out there.

I've followed the progress of Namibian rhino conservation for years. There has only been one report of a rhino found killed, and that by a local. Poachers from Zambia or South Africa, for instance, would have to cross the five hundred miles of Kalahari and Namib Desert to get at these rhinos. Distance from danger is the hallmark of their success.

Just over an hour after our cheetah sighting we found ourselves standing on the beach at Cape Crossing, looking at the largest fur seal colony in the world. In the nineteenth century the brown fur seals in this colony were estimated at six million animals. By the early twentieth century the colony was down to about one-half million. At the beginning of the twenty-first century the colony is estimated at between three-and-a-half and four million seals. They sleep in their own piss and the resulting stink is unbelievable. There is a constant onshore breeze blowing onto the beach. Our Maasai friends were particularly offended. Nonetheless, they wanted their pictures taken with the seals. Fred explained that fur seals are not seals at all; they are a variety of sea lion, very sharp-toothed predators. We didn't get too close, composing our pictures with the seals in the background.

The most fun I had all day was watching the Masaai hike up their skirts and wade into the ocean. We failed to tell them the water temperature was about 50 degrees Fahrenheit. They jumped up and down like they had a cobra underfoot. That lasted for about thirty seconds and then they hauled out like a pack of seals, only better smelling.

After eating lunch by the seashore in Swakamund, we headed to Windhoek. Finally, after a week we were back on a tar road. The road was so smooth I was napping when we turned into a native craft market near Usakos. Hearing that the dealers were all selling minerals, I woke up instantly. After I'd examined every specimen—holding us up for a half hour—I finally bought three beautiful black tourmalines (schorl) and a whopping terminated light blue topaz, notable for its size (more than half a kilo, or roughly 2,500 carats) and natural blue. All the specimens originated in the famous Erongo mountain district. The ladies selling the stuff knew their minerals. From goshenite to beta quartz and sodalite, they correctly identified every specimen. Only after we got back on the road did it occur to me that Aino was very annoyed. She thought buying a mineral specimen would be like buying an orange and only take thirty seconds. *So kill me, I held up the caravan.*

Mike and I saw the Tanzanian contingency off at the airport. Christopher, Sailenyi, and Kibiriti all invited me to their villages. Kibiriti and I were standing off to the side when he hugged me. I was kinda smooshed up against his chest since he stood almost a foot taller than me. He shyly whispered, "When you visit me there will be a shield and two spears waiting for you—one of them will be stuck in the sand outside your hut."

I looked up at him with affection. "Kibiriti," I said, "I'm happily married!"

He burst out laughing. Over my head, he repeated the conversation to the other Maasai in Ma. They all started laughing.

Kibiriti let go of me. "Eddie, a spear outside a hut means there is a warrior inside."

He has killed three lions in his time. His Maasai spear stands about six feet tall, but it is not thrown; it is used as a stabbing weapon like the Zulu assegai. Can you imagine getting about three feet from a lion before you strike it?

On my next trip to Arusha I will give myself at least four, if not five, weeks. I want to visit Christopher's village near Lake Natron as well as Kibiriti's near Tarangire National Park. Besides climbing Kilimanjaro, I want to climb Lingai, the soda carbonate volcano near Natron. My bucket list keeps growing!

Mike and I put up at a new bed and breakfast called the Olive Garden. We took Sunday off and traveled fifteen minutes out of Windhoek to a small national park called Valljoen. After driving the tar road from one end to the other in fewer than ten minutes, I was convinced there wasn't much there.

We backtracked toward the entrance, trying every dirt path. The dirt paths were not marked and the "map" was something produced by a third grader. In that way, we found the employee housing.

Finally, after several false turns we found the barely visible four-wheel drive trail across the park. Mike asked, "Should we take this, do you think?" Before I could think up a snide remark, off we went. In about two hours—and even during midday when most animals are not terribly active—we saw every animal in the park except cheetah. Let's see, I think it was fourteen gemsbok, about forty wildebeest, twelve Hartmann's mountain zebra, five springbok, ten warthogs, and one kinda old red hartebeest. Not bad game viewing at a park from which you can see the city.

During our last two days in Namibia we visited a half-dozen NGOs and the MET office. We revisited a couple of folks we met at our first day's meetings plus several other new contacts. I think we got the whole story of Namibia's CBNRM programs and problems. The worm in the apple is the government land ministry. They are on a path of settlement, disregarding community rights. As the land minister is certain to be the next president, it doesn't bode well for developing better property rights protection for communal or private lands. We can only hope that these corrupt politicians don't take Namibia down the Zimbabwean path of destruction.

We met several tourists at the bed and breakfast, including a young English couple who had all their money and papers in a backpack and were robbed at "screwdriver" point. The British consulate treated them pretty shabbily, but they finally got things straightened out and headed home. They were your typical young international travelers and surely won't make the same mistake twice. Never carry your valuables on your person, especially not all in one place. Wear trousers with double close pockets and spread your goods out across as many pockets as possible. Make sure you carry a copy of your passport—not your original—and keep it separate and secured. If you are carrying a handbag, carry it across your body and inside an outer jacket.

I've twice had someone try to pick my pocket and fail. At the infamous Madrid flea market notorious for Gypsy pickpockets, a place I had no business being (sounded like fun to me . . .), a small flock of guys tried the coin trick. If you have figured me out by now, you won't be surprised to hear that I studied up on pickpocket tricks before I ever hit the backstreets in Europe. So, when a Gypsy threw some small coins at my feet and tried to bowl me over, I instantly started backing up to the nearest wall, shouting at the top of my lungs, "pickpocket, pickpocket!" Two other guys crowded in and the guy behind me tried to get the wallet out of my back pocket. Since he was faced with Velcro over a zipper he didn't have time to score before the gatos descended on him in force. If they had caught the gang they would have done them some serious harm.

I've never been robbed in Africa, but Clive had his handbag lifted out of the back of his Toyota once when we were standing around waiting for our wives to purchase art supplies. My bag was locked in the cab and hidden under a seat. I had close to $10,000 in it.

CHAPTER 11

Back to Senuko Ranch

I MADE MY FIFTH TRIP to Zimbabwe in November 2004. I brought Jackie and we threw a big party at Mary Ann's—a *braai*, as the Zimbos call a barbeque. Raoul, Natasha, and the whole rhino team attended. The next day, Mike drove us to Senuko Ranch for our first extended stay with Lin and Clive.

It was summer in the Lowveld. The Lowveld has a two-part climate that is distinctly different from what we experience in the temperate United States. The climate has a winter and summer, combined with overlapping wet and dry seasons. Winter follows the end of an uncomfortably hot and wet season. It is mostly dry and relatively cool, but as summer approaches in September and October, the cool is succeeded by dry, hot weather. That's why the height of the African tourist season occurs during our American fall.

As the heat returns, the water holes dry up, forcing the game to become more and more concentrated. But the heat can be very intense. After days of dry heat exceeding 110 degrees, the rains finally come. Unfortunately they do not bring cooler temperatures. Rain and 110-degree heat is unbearable. To make matters worse, it signals the beginning of malaria season.

You can understand why we try to plan our visits for between May and the middle of August.

Even in winter, the weather can be very strange. One moment you're basking in 85-degree weather, with nighttime lows in the 50s, and the next thing you know a *guti* has arrived out of the south bringing with it temps in the 40s with fog and drizzle, sometimes lasting for several days. These are the days when you go swap your shorts and bush shirts for heavy winter fleece overnight.

We managed to miss schizophrenic weather this year. It was beautiful while we attended meetings of the conservancy members and traveled the conservancy from south to north and from the western boundaries with the communal areas to the Save River on the east. We also met with Conservancy Conservator Graham to learn more about their methodology and documentation of their wildlife conservation.

Mike had to get back to Harare after only a couple of days, so Clive took over as our chauffeur. Jackie immediately took to Lin Barrie who, in addition to being a famous wildlife painter, is an African painted dog fanatic. Jackie and Lin spent their days driving around the countryside in a Land Cruiser and painting *en plein air*.

The ancient baobab trees are an outstanding feature of Save Valley Conservancy. Since the elephants had been exterminated as early as the 1950s, the baobabs are in excellent condition. You see, during severe drought elephants eat the trunk of the baobab for its water content. Baobabs don't have heartwood like other deciduous trees. Their insides are composed of long, stringy, fibrous woody strands that act as a vast reservoir of water for the extended droughts. Baobabs can hold as much as 100,000 liters of water. I've seen what is left of the baobabs following a drought—nothing but a scattered mess of bark and limbs.

There was one particular baobab near the Senuko Lodge that Jackie and Lin liked to park under. It was nicknamed the "Absolut baobab." I suspect that you'd have to be pretty smashed on vodka before it would begin to look like an Absolut bottle, but who am I to argue?

Baobab seeds are carried in lovely gourd-like pods that rattle when dry. The seeds inside are sweet, tart, and full of vitamin C. It's rare to find one on the ground. All the animals covet them.

I got curious as to what a young baobab looks like. They are so nondescript that it took three years before a botanist finally pointed one out

One of the largest baobab trees in Africa, Senuko Ranch, Save Valley Conservancy, 2004.

to me. It was about four feet tall at about twenty years old and didn't look anything like a baobab. It looked like a tall, skinny stick, with some branches randomly pointing out the sides this way and that.

We were at the ranch about four days when, over the conservancy radio, Clive got a call from Raoul du Toit.

"Hi Clive, we've just landed at Malilangwe to translocate two white rhinos. Do you think Ed would like to join us?"

Would Ed like to join us? Duh! We jumped in the Land Cruiser and within an hour we had arrived at the staging area for the rhino operation. Raoul would fly his Husky and John McTaggart would fly his personal Robinson 44 helicopter with the veterinarian, Chris Foggins, hanging out the open side.

John, our helicopter pilot, is an enormous man, six foot five and 250 pounds. He is a Zimbabwean who was born in Britain (he holds a British passport), so he lives in multiple worlds. With his degree in agricultural engineering he went to work, right out of university, for his father-in-law, the owner of large tobacco plantations. He got bored quickly and switched his career to mining. Before the bad times, John operated chromium mines for foreign and domestic firms, enabling him to buy his own helicopter and do what he loves best—work on rhino conservation.

As we drove up, I spotted an enormous lorry with two shipping containers on the flatbed just off the airstrip. The rhino transport containers had been modified by the addition of doors to one end and the removal of the top, which was replaced by crossbeams and heavy metal mesh.

Natasha Anderson spotted Clive and me and walked over. I had met Natasha at Barberton Lodge in 2000 and then again at one of my Bombers of Beer parties. To me, she resembles a young Sigourney Weaver (if Sigourney Weaver were ever to be seen in nasty green coveralls).

"Hi Ed, we've got a job for you," she said with a glint in her eye and her arm around me. I expected to be put to work pulling on a rope or hauling gear around.

"We want you to fly spotter with Raoul."

"Uh, no way! I'm not trained to ID animals from the air!"

"Don't worry, Ed, you'll do just fine." Damn, I couldn't say no.

Loading a rhino transport container onto a lorry.

Raoul showed me how to climb in the Husky without hurting myself. Imagine worming your way into a sharp-edged, metal trunk raised four feet off the ground—that's what it's like to climb into the backseat of the two-seat Husky. Then he had to show me how to wriggle into the five-point seat belt–shoulder harness rig. It would take me at least another five years of practice to get it right on my own. Then there was the headset with its voice-activated microphone that you have

Interior shot of the Husky spotter plane, Sierra Oscar. Note the size of the back seat!

to place right on your lip. Getting comfortable in the Husky is just not a possibility. But I didn't care—I was going rhino spotting.

The scouts reported sighting a big, old white rhino. Up we went! McTaggart and Foggins followed us in the chopper.

Five minutes later, I spotted him. I saw him before Raoul! Wow!

In came the helicopter. I was expecting something from *Animal Planet*. You know, rhino running, helicopter flying low alongside. Vet shoots tranquilizer from twenty feet.

Nope! The 'copter never got closer than one hundred meters, the rhino having been found in a fairly open grassy area called a *vlei*. Raoul and I flew in circles above the rhino. I waited and waited for the helicopter to make its move. I never saw the shot, but finally the rhino just kinda sat down.

Rhinos are darted with the sedative etorpine, or M99, a semisynthetic opioid. M99 is called a "dangerous drug" by large animal veterinarians for a good reason: It is fatal to humans from as little contact as a drop on the skin. A large beast like this white rhino was hit with at least six CCs. That's enough to kill twelve hundred grown men.

The animal is almost always darted in its enormous butt, a lovely target, I grant you. Often, some of the M99 leaks out of the syringe. So, working around the butt end of a rhino is really dangerous. You can't afford to make a mistake around M99. A few years later they invited me to take the "Dangerous Drugs" course. I declined. I come out once a year. I'm not about to handle that shit.

We zipped back to the airstrip. We landed and jumped in a Land Cruiser. Within ten minutes we were alongside the rhino. Raoul was working the winch on the lorry and I was behind a 5,000-pound rhino preparing to push it into the container. The crew put a rope around its neck and threaded it through a bolt-hole in the container. About eight scouts were on the far end of the rope and would pull.

Chris had already put a hypodermic in the rhino's ear loaded with the reversal drug. About six of us gathered around and lifted the enormous head. The container was lowered down and shifted over until the rhino's chin was resting on the edge of the container.

Chris walked all around, came back to the rhino's rear end and finally said, "all ready?" I wondered what was going to happen next.

Chris pressed the plunger on the reversal drug, diprenorphine and, holding an electric cattle prod, watched the rhino for signs of it waking up. *Whoosh,* the rhino let out a huge deep breath. Then it sighed. It wiggled and tried to lift a front foot. Then it tried to stand up.

"Let's go," Chris cried, and hit the rhino's hind foot with the cattle prod. Once, twice, and on the third shock, the rhino raised a front leg and started to take a step forward. All six of us on the ass-end pushed as hard as we could. The rhino got up and walked right into the container. Two of the team leapt forward and closed the steel doors. Piece of cake!

My first relocation would turn out to be the easiest I ever saw.

—

For several years I wondered about my "first job" with Rhino Ops. Finally, three years later, while we were all staying at Senuko Lodge, I asked Natasha about that first day. We had just finished a very long day, working from about 5:30 a.m. until 8 p.m. Following our normal routine, we had cleaned up and immediately afterward hit the bar. We were pretty well loaded when I finally asked her about the first day I flew spotter.

"Ed," she said, putting her arm around me and looking down (so, I'm short, what of it?). "Graham Connear (primary spotter for Rhino Ops back then) couldn't make it that day, so it fell to me to spot for Raoul. I get airsick. I figured that barfing on my boss wouldn't help my career and you getting airsick would get you out of my hair—permanently."

"Ha!" I said. "You didn't know that I don't get airsick. I don't get seasick. I love little airplanes. Raoul could fly in circles for six hours and it wouldn't bother me."

"Well, I know it now." And then she kissed me.

On that first op, we had the second rhino loaded by 3 p.m. We had to transport the rhinos two hours to the boma. We convoyed from Malilangwe to the center of Save Valley Conservancy. The vet and a game scout sat on top of the containers to monitor the health of the two rhinos. By dark, the rhinos were settled in their own individual enclosures. We returned to Senuko for showers, scotch, and dinner (in that order).

CHAPTER 12

The Geriatric Fire Brigade

A FEW DAYS LATER, MANY of us had gone in different directions after finishing up a few business meetings. John had flown off to Gweru in the helicopter, Romeo Lima Zulu, that morning. Most of the lodge staff had driven into Chiredzi to participate in a rugby match—typical Sunday. Only a handful of folks were around, mostly scouts enjoying a day off at "home" and us guys, including Lin's father, Arthur, a retired mapmaker with the Rhodesian Geological Survey.

Clive's accountant, Tom Taylor, who had driven down for the meetings, was just about to leave for the five-hour drive back to Harare when a call came in over the wireless.

"Alpha One, Alpha One, this is Senuko Four, there's a fire heading toward the lodge."

Squatters on the southwest corner of the conservancy had decided to burn their maize field on a day when the wind was howling in from the west. The fire raced across the savanna and mopane forest at something like thirty miles an hour.

With the main workforce watching or playing rugby in the nearest town, Chiredzi, about an hour away, we needed to round up all the warm bodies we could find. Clive gathered me, Tom, and Arthur, and I immediately dubbed us the Geriatric Fire Brigade—our average age was sixty-something.

We rounded up another six game scouts who didn't have the day off. Thomas, Senuko's head safari guide, took a second vehicle and gathered another six who were working elsewhere.

Gordon, Clive's nephew and one of his professional hunters, drove to the airstrip and took off in his micro light. When I talk about these guys being either heroic or crazy, I mean it. Gordon flew over the fire from about 3 p.m. until three seconds before dark—in an airplane composed of glorified tent poles and a tarp and powered by a lawnmower engine.

I knew virtually nothing about fighting a wildfire. Tom and Arthur had limited experience as well. No matter, the Geriatric Fire Brigade drove around the fire and fearlessly attacked it from behind. We drove right though the burn, breathing acrid choking smoke, fire crackling around the tires.

Clive rushed around the front of the fire and stopped directly ahead of it. If you could have seen the fire from the air, it would have looked something like an arrowhead pointed straight at Senuko Lodge.

We drove to the intersection of the "B" line road and an old fence line road. Clive called Thomas on the shortwave. Within minutes Thomas drove up and dropped the guys off a few meters back from the intersection. That point was going to be the apex of our fire line.

The dozen or so of us "firefighters" assembled behind the vehicles. Everybody but me immediately ran to the nearest bushes and cut or snapped off a big stick with green leaves covering the distal end. I got handed one. That would be our tool for beating out hot spots that might cross our fire line. This was not going to be a high-tech operation!

I was about to learn how to use a dirt road as a firebreak, setting up back-burns between the advancing fire and the road to control the fire's advance. The other guys were already cutting and ripping up dead grass to use as firebrands. I got with the program.

Thomas lit a fire at the intersection of two roads. We split into two groups, dragging the burning brand in the grass along the edge of the road. As the guy with the burning brand tossed it away before it burned the shit out of him, another guy stepped up and lit his. We quickly moved along the road, leapfrogging each other as we spread the fire down the line. After a few minutes, I stood back with my switch and watched to make sure embers didn't fire up behind us. Our method worked so well that not a single spot fire managed to cross the road. The back-burn burned sideways and back toward the main fire, which was moving fast toward us.

Clive yelled at me. I couldn't hear his shout for the roar of the fire. Somebody nearer yelled. I walked . . . then ran, back to the truck. The Geriatric Fire Brigade stuffed our branches and ourselves into the Land Cruiser and tore off to the north to try to flank the fire. We cut grass, lit our brands, and worked along the road. After twenty minutes of this, Clive rounded us up again and drove us further along the fire's flank. Dropping us off, he left the three of us behind.

"Just work slowly down this road and I'll be back in a little while." Clive turned the truck around and was gone in the smoke.

I looked at the more distant smoke of the main fire. Could I see the fire out there? I wasn't sure. We seemed to be on one flank. Tom, Arthur, and I got to work. The fire was really hot. The smoke choked you. We played leapfrog with the burning brands. I kept burning my hand and wrist.

"Man this is hot work and painful too," I said to Arthur, coming up behind me with a fresh brand.

"Why don't you try holding the brand right-handed? You keep sticking your left hand into the fire. Haven't you noticed, we're working left to right?" So much dyslexia, so little awareness!

I spotted a leopard tortoise, ran into the scrub, and rescued it. The other two had continued to extend the back-burn. I had to run around them, the tortoise squirming in my hands.

This isn't so bad, I told myself.

Just then the wind changed direction. We saw the flames of the main fire flare up maybe ten meters high. It was headed right for us from maybe a couple of hundred meters away. We were no longer on the flank. A freight train of fire, along a front maybe a kilometer wide, was bearing down on us. If we didn't get protection from a back-burn we would be fried. The geriatrics mobilized. As fast as we could cut grass, as fast as we could light fire, we raced down that dirt road, fortunately, at a slight angle away from the fire's front. We lit a kilometer of continuous backfire in about fifteen minutes, finally turning a corner where we intercepted another dirt road, effectively cutting off the fire's advance. I was actually panting, we had moved so fast!

As we finished up at the corner, I watched the fire bear down and combine with the back-burn further up the road. We had done it! It just remained to walk back up through choking smoke and beat out the little remaining fires that were doing their best to burn leaves and cross the road.

Backfire lit by the Geriatric Fire Brigade, 2004.

Clive showed up with the vehicle. We all jumped in and drove back toward the original fire line. The back-burn had done its job. It was now 5 p.m. In two hours the team had back-burned nine kilometers of road and contained a fire that burned about six hundred hectares of grass and woodland. None of the standing trees and very few of the shrubs had been killed. Already-felled mopane and leadwood logs on the ground would smolder for several weeks, but the fire was contained. We drove back along the perimeter.

"I've been in touch with Gordon. The back of the fire needs some work, but the front and flanks are completely contained," Clive informed us. "We'll drive around and work the back for a while." Clive drove for a while and then got on the radio with Gordon. We headed away from the fire. Tom spoke up.

"Clive, won't the fire come this way?"

"Not unless the wind shifts to the east of north and that's unlikely. I think we've done it. We deserve a sundowner in peace."

I thought to myself, *Wouldn't want to miss our evening beer just because a couple of square miles is still burning right behind us!*

We drove away from the burn area and came to a large open area of umbrella acacia and acacia scrub. In an opening about 150 meters across, near the remains of a very old kopje composed of worn down granite, we'd drink our beers. There were impala in the distance, but not many other animals. They had fled the fire.

"Sometimes we find cheetah out here, relaxing after a day of hunting. But not tonight," said Clive.

We opened our beers African style (one bottle cap against another bottle cap), except for me, that is, I used my Swiss Army knife. We munched on dried orange slices and watched the sunset. The sun was blood red from the smoke. I tried photographing it over the top of the acacias, but it was difficult to get the exposure right.

Clive reminisced. "We were having a sundowner right here one evening. It got dark quite suddenly, as it is wont to do in the tropics. The clients were standing right over there." He pointed to a spot not much more than ten feet from where we stood, drinking.

"Our tracker walked around to the left side of the vehicle and pulled out a spotlight. He shined it past the clients. To my horror, a pride of lions had sneaked up on us. They were sitting on their haunches just ten meters away, mind you, watching us. I couldn't tell if they were curious or choosing snacks. Fortunately, the clients kept their cool and I got them to slowly, ever so nonchalantly saunter over to the vehicle and climb in. Lucky for us the lions never moved."

Later that night, right around 8 p.m., the wind shifted to southwesterly. Within two hours, the flames that had lit the night sky were completely knocked down. The wind shift had allowed what remained of the fire to burn back on itself.

—

Upon our return to Harare, I had a job for Mike—something he was totally unprepared for. You see, in the spring of 2004, the Denver Botanic Gardens hosted a show of Chapungu stone sculptures from Zimbabwe. The pieces were marvelous. I discovered that Chapungu was just ten minutes from where I was staying with Mary Ann and Mike on Kings Road, in the Queen Anne district of Harare. Mike, being a wildlife biologist, not an art critic, didn't even know the Chapungu Sculpture Park was nearby. So, when we got back from the Lowveld I had a plan in mind. Well, sort of.

"Mike, please drive me over to Chapungu. I have directions." I explained what I knew about the Chapungu Sculpture Park.

"What the devil? You want to look at stone carvings?" asked Mike, more than a little incredulous.

"No, I want to buy sculptures and ship them to Denver."

"Uh, huh. Well, it'll be a cock-up for sure, but let's give it a go."

So, off we went to find the sculptors at a run-down, wide spot in a clearing, with a little brick building on one side. There were half a dozen men and women engaged in stone carving.

I picked out four sculptures weighing between 100 and 550 pounds. I paid the artists in US dollars. The money would save their families from hyperinflation for a year.

When I was done making my selections and paying, I said, "Great, ship them to this address."

"We can't ship, we don't know how," said Nhamo Chamutsa. Nicolas and Benjamin nodded their heads in agreement.

"Okay, no problem. I'll be back shortly."

Mike and I drove back to Mary Ann's. I opened the phone book. It didn't take more than a dozen calls to the wrong people before I found a real, live shipper. I arranged for the pickup. The sculptures would be trucked from Chapungu to the rail station, then travel by rail to Natal, South Africa. At Natal, they would be placed in a container to make the

One of the Chapungu sculptures I purchased in Harare.

trip from Natal to Antwerp, Belgium, and then transshipped to New York. The final leg would be by semitrailer to Denver. Piece of cake!

Mike and I drove back to Chapungu. "Hi guys, I've got the shipper coming day after tomorrow. Box up your sculptures."

"We have no boxes, Eddie," all three chimed in together.

"No problem. We'll be back in a little while."

Mike and I drove to a hardware/lumber yard and bought everything necessary to box up and protect four stone sculptures. We dropped off the materials. Of course, I paid the three artists to build the boxes.

Almost five months later, I got a call from a shipping firm in Antwerp. "Mr. Warner, we have four boxes directed to you at this address. If you don't wire us the shipping fees immediately, we'll dump it all in the harbor."

"Wait a second, the bill of lading is COD."

"We couldn't care less."

"Okay, but tomorrow is a national holiday. Please give me five days. You'll get your money."

Three weeks later I got a call from the shipper at New York harbor.

"We have these boxes with your name on it. Customs requires they be X-rayed. The cost is $250. If you don't wire the money . . ."

"Just give me the wiring instructions, and you'll have the money tomorrow," I responded.

Another week had gone by when I received a call from a bonded warehouse near Denver International Airport. "Mr. Warner, we have these crates addressed to you. Who is your agent?"

"Why would I need an agent?"

"To process your boxes through customs, of course," answered the puzzled young lady.

"Can I do this myself?"

"Come on by and I'll help you fill out the forms," she said helpfully.

The next day I processed my sculptures through customs and homeland security. The bozo at HS looked at the papers, looked at me, then asked, "What were you doing in Zimbabwe?"

If you can't imagine rudeness elevated to the level of art, you have never dealt with one of these gummint bureau-craps.

I looked at him, smiled, and said, "I was wandering around Harare on my vacation and came across these stone carvings, so I bought them."

"Oh, very well. Here is your release from bond."

The sculptures now stand in a place of prominence in my courtyard. They weren't difficult to install. With the help of my best friend, Daniel, a hippy carpenter turned high-end cabinetmaker, it only took eight hours, a few ramps, covering for the floors and courtyard, a material lift, and the knowledge of knots I acquired when I was in the Boy Scouts.

CHAPTER 13

Mountain Biking in the Bush

I ARRIVED BACK IN HARARE in June 2005 with Jackie in tow. We had two big suitcases and a bicycle box precariously perched on top of the rest.

A bicycle box you say? I wasn't getting enough exercise during my visits to Africa. Walking on flat ground wasn't cutting it and the nearest "health club" was several hundred miles away. In Denver, I rode my mountain bike to work most days. I'd ride about thirty miles a day along Cherry Creek or the South Platte River for exercise. So, I packed up my Trek 600, a hand pump, and a half-dozen spare tubes.

"Where do you plan to ride this bike, anyway?" Jackie asked.

"Around the Save Valley Conservancy," I replied. "Think of all those dirt roads I can ride on."

"Think about all those wild animals that can (1) stomp you, and (2) eat you."

"Oh, honey, don't worry, the animals won't bother me," I answered.

At customs we loaded up our luggage on the rolling carts. Besides the bicycle box we had two very large red suitcases loaded with computers, GPS units, cameras, and other equipment. As I headed to the "Nothing to Declare" line, I looked up to the second floor windows where drivers and travel agents wait for their guests. I spotted Lin and Clive. Then I spotted several other friends. *How nice,* I thought, *they came by to welcome us.*

Actually, they were placing bets that we would never get through customs.

As I pushed the lead cart, a customs agent intercepted us.

"Excuse me, sir, what is in that large box?" They are nothing if not polite.

I immediately switched on my television-Texan accent: "Howdy there. Why, this here is my mountain bike. I've been on driving and walking safaris in your country. This time I'm gonna do a biking safari in the southeast."

"How old is your bike, sir?" the customs agent asked.

"Well, this here bike is about eight years old. I figgered if I bust it on my ride, well it'll be never no mind." *What the hell did I just say?*

The customs agent looked at me with supreme tolerance. "Have a nice time in our country."

Behind me, Jackie pushed about twenty grand of contraband through the line.

—

Once again we had arrived during Zimbabwean winter. We didn't remain in Harare at the onset, but traveled immediately down to Senuko Ranch in Clive and Lin's Toyota loaded with our gear, including my old mountain bike, about 30 pounds of books for Lin (wolves, coyotes, and other natural history), and a new Canon camera for Clive. He needed to replace the one Lin had run over with the Land Cruiser a couple of weeks earlier. I noticed a big, old "chigubu"—what we would call a "jerry can"—in the back.

"The country is completely out of fuel at the moment, Ed," acknowledged Clive, seeing my upturned eyebrows. "We got a tanker shipment in last week thanks to John [McTaggart, our other partner]. Without the

5,000 liters of diesel, we'd still be sitting at Senuko and you'd still be sitting at this empty airport."

"God, Clive, this happened when I was here in '03," I said.

"It's worse this time. No one will give the country any credit. On my return from the States, we were held up in London because Royal Dutch Shell wouldn't fill up the Air Zim plane on credit. They wanted cash!"

One of the indirect, positive consequences was the little to no traffic on the roads. I always scan for the positive, but I admit that's a little much.

When we reached the ranch, we unloaded the bike at the workshops. I stayed behind to supervise its reassembly. After the mechanic and I put together all the bits and pieces, I pedaled the five kilometers back to the lodge. There, waiting at the car park, stood Jackie, Lin, and Clive. I pedaled up and jumped off the bike. Lin handed me a two-way radio.

"You're now officially 'Echo Mobile.' Clive is 'Alpha One,' the Lodge is 'Senuko One,' and

Mike Jones filling his truck from a jerry can; the petrol station was empty, just a place to park. There was no petrol in the whole country that year.

I'm 'Senuko Two.' You are to carry the radio and," Lin paused for effect, "you are to keep the radio turned on whenever you're out on that bike!"

Clive handed me a .357 magnum revolver in a left-handed holster.

"What is this?" I asked Clive. "Is it a Smith & Wesson or a Ruger?"

I slipped the revolver out of its holster as I spoke and thumbed back the hammer. "Good Lord," I exclaimed, "it's a single action."

Clive mumbled some name, maybe "Jaguar," that I didn't really catch. I was mostly concerned about laying that trigger back down as carefully as I could. I flipped open the cylinder and spun it. All six chambers were charged with cartridges. I ejected one, spun the cylinder until the empty chamber rested under the hammer, snapped the cylinder shut, holstered the handgun, and handed the sixth cartridge to Clive.

Clive looked down at the round in the palm of his hand and said, "Ed, what if you need that sixth round?"

"Clive, in America we practice 'gun safety,' so we never leave a live round against the hammer. The standing joke in Alaska goes like this: After you shoot the bear five times, what use is a sixth round?

"If you need the sixth round it'll be to shoot yourself."

Each morning I would take off on the bike around 6:45 a.m. I didn't want to miss breakfast but wanted to ride in full light (so I didn't end up being breakfast!). It's amazing how many things you can do at once. I had to watch out for acacia thorn, potholes, pythons, and especially elephants, rhinos, and lions. That's multitasking at its essence!

Me getting ready to ride my bike on SVC; notice the radio on one hip, the .357 magnum on the other.

Elephants were my primary concern. A large breeding herd was hanging around camp during our whole stay. I'd see fresh spore and litter from branches every morning. Sometimes I'd find the remains of the plastic water pipes the elephants loved to dig up. They like clean water and can hear the pipes gurgling underground. Repairing PVC water pipe is a permanent occupation on the conservancy. I was careful not to bike up the rear end of a breeding herd and find myself between a momma and her baby.

Elephants are perfectly civilized if you give them a chance to do the right thing—well, most of the time. Climbing a tree to get away from a big elephant doesn't work. It can knock the tree down. The proper method of disentangling yourself from an elephant herd is to run away, tear your shirt off, and at just the right moment throw your shirt one way and run the other. Really, I'm serious. That's the theory. Elephants have poor eyesight but a great sense of smell. If you're lucky they will follow the direction of your stinky shirt! I'm loath to find myself in a situation to actually to test the theory.

One morning I came across the spore of an entire lion pride. There on the soft sand road were the fresh prints of four adult females, two subadults, and a big male. I studied the tracks for a while. They were definitely headed in the direction from which I had just come.

Hey, if I already passed them I might as well keep on going.

Later Clive asked me, "What would you have done if the tracks were going the other way?"

"I'd have turned around. I'm not crazy, you know? I'm not going to ride up the ass end of a pride of lions on purpose!"

Another day, I turned a corner and there ahead of me was a pile of steaming buffalo shit. I slid to a stop and climbed a tree. After surveying the countryside through my binoculars for the Cape buffalo, I shimmied on down and continued my ride. Those big old Cape buffalo bulls are called "dagga boys," and are a nightmare of hostility. They're not the kind of critter you want to encounter on a bicycle.

Several times on my adventures over the years, I've been sent up the nearest tree by what I thought was a rhino's snort. I learned that what I was hearing was actually a warning call from a zebra. It sounds exactly like a rhino to me. With all those rhinos around, the zebra has learned to sound the alarm unnoticed. Sure worked on me!

One day I whipped around a bend on a route with cover so dense that I was screened on both sides of the dirt road. As I finished the turn, maybe twenty-five meters up the road, was a big elephant bull with his trunk stretched way up in the air, plucking new growth off an umbrella acacia. I skidded to a stop. There was no chance to run away. But the elephant never looked at me. He kept on eating. Testing the wind, I realized I was downwind. So, I dismounted, walked the bike a hundred meters back from where I'd slid to a stop, and resumed watching him through my binoculars. He eventually walked off.

When I returned to the lodge, I described to Thomas what had happened. He laughed at me. "Eddie, he was chewing. Can you hear anything when you are chewing?" Such a simple explanation for why he left me alone. The bull never knew I was there.

"Better lucky than smart." That's my motto, and it seems to be true!

—

We had dinner that night at Lin and Clive's house along with Stephanie Romanich and Peter Lindsay, two wild dog researchers who had arrived earlier in the day in an old Jeep, which was gasping its last breath. Clive had them drop it at the ranch workshops and put his mechanics to fixing it. Stephanie, a young American, was the real field scientist of the pair. Peter, a Brit, was very good at writing professional papers, but he could barely tie his shoelaces.

Jackie jumped at the chance to help him dart an injured wild dog the next day. When they opened the front door of his Jeep (now repaired) to get on their way, his underwear fell out. It was downhill from there. He was never able to dart the dog. He couldn't shoot straight. Stephanie and Peter left the next day.

Jackie had us rolling on the floor with her retelling of how they approached the dog pack with Peter firing darts just about anywhere but in the direction of the target dog.

—

Lin and Clive live in a magical spot. Their house is a huge, two-story, thatched-roof affair sited on a low-lying kopje. Unusual for African homes, the kitchen—complete with professional propane range—is actually indoors. Regardless, most of the cooking takes place behind the kitchen at a fire pit. Lin is vegan, but what a cook! The rest of us ate game meat, warthog on this occasion, along with local yams, tomatoes, and greens.

During dinner Clive's three Jack Russell terriers went berserk, sending flowerpots flying amid a mad scramble. Jackie and I leapt up and went after them. Jackie excitedly screamed, "a kill, a kill," as we watched the female Jack Russell hold down the rat while Mici, her mate, delivered the crushing deathblow to its skull.

Back around the campfire, Clive grinned at Jackie. "I never would have guessed you were so bloodthirsty, my dear."

"It must be great having the dogs around for protection," she replied, apropos of nothing.

Clive grinned some more. "If ever they come running back here in the dark and leap into your lap, be prepared. They're liable to be followed by a leopard."

Before Jackie and I headed back to the lodge that night we passed back through the house. The floor was dotted with large white splashes. I looked at Clive. Lin answered my unspoken question: "We have barn owls nesting above the fireplace. They are out hunting just now, but they are raising four young."

I felt awful for their aged majordomo. That was a lot of bird shit to clean off the floors every day for three months!

We walked over to the fireplace, but couldn't hear a thing. We spotted the male barn owl sitting in the middle of the road as we pulled onto the main road to drive back to our chalet at the lodge.

"He looks like he owns the place," I said to Jackie and promptly swerved off the verge to avoid the owl.

—

The main objectives on this trip included reviewing the Africa conservation projects, finalizing my business deal with Clive, and throwing a party for my friends in Harare—a Fourth of July party at Mary Ann's house. Clive, Lin, Jackie, and I drove back to Harare a week before the party date.

Since Mary Ann was in Britain, I figured Mike could act as host, and Zimbabwean friends Kevin and Dawn could help. Mike got the permit for the fireworks display from the police and Kevin, who had to make a trip to Jo'burg for business, agreed to buy the explosives.

I quickly had second thoughts about shooting off fireworks. I kept having this nightmare vision of the Zimbabwean Army streaming over the walls to quell the attempted revolution. I also had to change my plan to hand-churn ice cream. There was no fresh cream to be had in the country, the dairy industry having been destroyed by Mugabe's "Land Reform."

Before I could purchase anything I had to find some cash. You don't go to an ATM machine in Zimbabwe. You don't even go to the bank. So I tapped into the informal currency exchange of friends, who gladly traded me ten million in Zim dollars, in packets of ten thousand- and twenty thousand-dollar bills, for my US dollars at the black market rate of about 85¢ per $10,000. Bricks of money in central African countries are made up in blocks of bills bound with a paper clip securing a last bill folded over the rest.

With Zim dollars in hand, I went to the grocery store to buy the ice cream. I paid the clerk and drove away. About two minutes later, a little light bulb went on (or someone hit the panic button in my brain). I pulled out the wad of bills and counted an individual stack. I had paid her twice the cost of the ice cream. The stack didn't contain a hundred thousand dollars as I'd thought. It contained two hundred thousand. Just as I started to throw a fit my math skills engaged. I may have paid double, but the poor grocery clerk (poor in money, not creativity!) had just got a tip of about $8 US. I calmly went back to shopping.

The party guests were mostly scientists from World Wildlife Fund or other NGOs, consultants, and Zim friends I'd made on my many visits. They seemed to be quite amused by the idea of celebrating American

Independence Day in Harare, the capital of the worst fascist state in Africa. Okay, maybe not fascist, but certainly the worst "gangster government," to borrow a phrase from George Ayittey's *Africa Unchained* (Palgrave McMillan, 2005).

All I really cared about was being able to say "up the British" without offending anyone.

Among the guests were most of the WWF rhino project personnel. You will recall I had met Raoul du Toit, the project head, in 2000 and had worked with him since 2003. The rhino meant more to Raoul that anything or anyone. Perhaps he feels a kinship with the prehistoric, lumbering beasts: Raoul is built close to the ground and has a high forehead. I like Raoul a lot, and his stubborn dedication is respected by friends and enemies alike.

Natasha, whom I had met during my first rhino op, was also at my party. She was now second in command of the rhino project. As bad as I wanted to be invited to work on another rhino rescue with them, I knew it was futile. They were working in the Midlands, three hundred miles from where I would be staying in the Lowveld. So, I figured the only way to impress them with my good intentions was to continue to fill them with bombers of beer.

The party was a great success; no one wanted to leave. We marched around following fifes and drums. We all shouted "Up the British" with great gusto. We all sang "Yankee Doodle Dandy." All the food was eaten, except the salads. It seems that Zim wildlife biologists are carnivores! Fortunately, we never ran out of beer. The only friends that didn't show up turned out to be the few expats and locals who couldn't get their hands on any petrol. You gotta have connections!

—

Clive and I had a very productive meeting about our partnership. Previously, we had agreed that I would become an invisible partner. The Zim government could have made Clive's life miserable if they found out he was in business with a Yank. That changed during this trip, at least for the moment. I was now the showcase foreign investor. I met three different ministers or cabinet members and the head of National Parks.

I'm sure my calling everyone by first names is dead wrong in this very socially conscious society. Trouble is, I have my own set of rules. First names first. It's always been that way with me and always will. My friends can only hope I never run into the president or the pope. (I've since run into four presidents and two prime ministers. I've called all of them by their first names: "Hi Bill, I'm Ed, and this is Jackie.") Clive proved once again to be mighty restrained.

—

We were invited to have an early morning meeting with Charles Davy. I had met him in 2000 at his conservancy of, oh, 850,000 acres, on the Bubye River northwest of Beitbridge, about 125 miles west of the Save Valley. As we were driving to his house in Harare, Clive filled me in on recent gossip. "Ed, have you ever met Charles's daughter, the stately blonde Chelsea?"

"No, Charles was alone when I flew to Bubye with Karl [Hess, Jr.], and Guy [Barber]."

"Well, she's dating Prince Harry and they are visiting her dad at the moment."

"Now, Clive, you don't think I'm going to run into His Royal Highness this morning and just walk right up to him and say, 'Hi Harry, how the hell are ya? I'm Ed?'"

"Mmph, mmph, mumble, mumble." (That's what Clive sounds like when he's perturbed but doesn't want to say anything uncivilized.)

I've recounted this exchange to friends who assure me that Harry would have found my style quite amusing.

"Not to worry, Clive. Maybe they'll be sleeping in," I reassured him.

Just my luck—they were off partying in some other part of the country during our visit.

Charles confirmed that having sole control (outvoting his partners with his majority interest) of Bubye, doing really good community outreach, and fostering community participation (and being rich and powerful), had all contributed to keeping Mugabe's government from stealing his land. I was most interested in the corporate structure of Charles's management scheme.

In 2000, when I first visited, I speculated that the conservancies that would survive would be the ones with strong governance, real constitutions, solidarity of purpose, and good community relations. Five years later, my speculation had proven to be true. I had data from four private land conservancies. The weakest, the Gwayi Conservancy, managed by a group of individual, Boer game ranchers each doing their own thing, had failed. Chris Van Wyk, Russell's father-in-law, was the last of two dozen farmers to be forced off. Fifty thugs with shotguns finally convinced the tough old man to leave his ranch. Subsequently, politicians have oversold hunting rights to rapacious South African professional hunters, effectively allowing the rape of the land. Two decades of conservation down the drain.

On a scale of strongest to weakest governing model, Charles's Bubye Conservancy is only bested by Paul Tudor Jones's Malilangwe Conservancy, which isn't even owned by whites. Jones placed the whole kit and caboodle in a community trust, thus protecting it from Mugabe's indigenization plan. Hell, it's already indigenized. That Paul is a very clever man.

The Save Valley Conservancy, on the strong side of middle, has survived due to good governance. For instance, besides a solid constitution, they set up a community trust to the benefit of the local people. Clive, with a history of collaboration and fair-trading with the local Shangaan people, total resistance to government demands for dismembering the conservancy, and a high profile with international conservation groups, has kept Save Valley Conservancy virtually intact.

The Bubiana Conservancy was near the middle of the scale, until it was dismantled in pieces due to poor cooperation among farmers and a policy of compromise with the gangster government. Only the head guy, Ken Drummond, is left. His neighbors all feel like he sold them out by trading their properties to protect his. He was in bed with Mugabe.

Following meetings with National Parks, we loaded back up for the return to Senuko Ranch. Besides riding my bike like an idiot, we'd arranged for Mike Jones to come down so that we could tour the northern section of Gonarezhou National Park. An Intensive Protection Zone (IPZ) had been proposed for that area that would include the reintroduction of rhinos. Clive had proposed that we petition the government for a concession in this area, to include setting up a trust and, among other things, installing private game scouts. At that time there were widespread rumors, some decidedly true, that National Parks scouts were among the most flagrant poachers.

CHAPTER 14

Broken Down in Gonarezhou

THE FIVE OF US PILED into one of the Senuko Lodge Land Cruisers, the type with an open top and two levels of seats raised above the driving area. I sat with Clive. Mici, the boss's Jack Russell terrier, sat in my lap to keep me warm. Lin and Jackie sat behind us and Mike sat in the back where he could stretch out his artificial leg.

We stopped at Chilo Gorge Lodge and checked in with the staff. We then crossed the Save River at Mahenye Camp and headed southeast toward the Runde (or Lundi, depending on which way a mzungu transliterated Ndebele) River. Both of these safari lodges are owned by Clive (and me and John, I suppose), built on land rented from the Mahenye community that lives just on the other side of the river from Gonarezhou National Park.

Driving onto the river's floodplain, I was certain we would get stuck. Remember, I'm an old field geologist. I pretty much know all the different ways you can "stick" a four-wheel drive.

Loose sand is notoriously difficult to drive on. It just flings everywhere as the tire spins. When we stopped at the top of an elephant crossing, I jumped out and locked the hubs. Yep, that's right. Part of the charm of a Land Cruiser is its manual locking hubs—just like in the old days of my

International Scouts. None of this push-button stuff you find in a fancy SUV! Clive stuck the truck in high four-wheel drive. We ground down to the sand and started across. Then a wheel started to slip.

Uh, oh, I thought. *I hope we have a shovel.*

Clive shifted the transfer case into low range and slipped the clutch as the engine idled. We rocked backward for a second or two. Then, he shifted into low gear. The big old Land Cruiser rocked forward and got going.

That's the best damn four-wheel driving I've ever seen, I said to myself.

As it turned out, we crossed the riverbed easily enough, but the abandoned campground had been thoroughly trashed by elephants. Downed and shredded acacias and African ivory nut palm covered a lot of vague road tracks. Finding our way was difficult. We drove through the bush, on and off track for the better part of an hour. Finally, Clive recognized a track that had been used no less than three years earlier and we hit the highway. Well, the road, which had been used at least once or twice this year, certainly felt like a highway! We headed more or less southwest out of the river valley and into a wonderland of scattered teak and high yellow grass.

"Where's the game, Clive?" Even with the poaching in the park, I was surprised to find no animals on the plain.

Clive pointed to the single watering hole. It was dry. "No diesel to run the pump, thus no water, Ed." The water was piped in from a borehole five kilometers away. "Game has to walk ten kilometers from the river to graze on that lovely grass." It was too far, and by midday, none were to be seen.

We continued to drive higher and higher until we came to the backside of the Chilojo Cliffs. Red and buff layers of sandstone and "grits"—coarser grain than sand that we Yanks call conglomerate—give the pinnacles and lonely points a cheery aspect. These sandstones of the Lower Karoo Formation of Permian Age sit atop the Precambrian basement granites and were exposed by the erosion of the ancient granitic mountains.

*Looking down on the Runde River from the Chilobo cliffs: Lin Barrie, wildlife
artist, left; my wife, Jackie, Clive Stockil (French Order of Merit, 2011,
Prince William Award, 2013); & Mike Jones, right.*

From the rim we looked down on the Runde River and Clive's old
camp, a river we would cross again in the vicinity of Fishans Camp—the
place I had visited and camped overnight two years earlier with Russell
Gammon. After a spell of picture taking, we hopped back in the Cruiser
and hauled southward to round the cliffs and approach the river. We
radioed Chilo Lodge with our position before we left. That turned out
to be a really good idea. A half hour later, I recognized the roads leading
to the campsites. I knew the intersection by its one-and-one-half-meter-
square, green-painted concrete block with road names on its sides. Today,
the block was upside down—turned over by busy elephants.

Our plan was to eat a picnic lunch at Fishans before crossing a ford in
the river. We would have to ford because Cyclone Ilene washed away the
impossibly beautiful bridge that had spanned the river until 2000.

Still a couple of kilometers from the campsite, we heard a grinding noise coming from under the bonnet (that's African English for hood) of the Land Cruiser. Clive hit the brakes and we jumped out to see what was under the vehicle. We expected to find a branch caught in a belt or something similar and fixable. There were lots of thorny acacia branches under there, but nothing interfering with a belt. We drove on.

Another kilometer of progress and the grinding got worse. We pulled into the campsite and raised the bonnet. Sparks erupted. Clive cut the ignition and we checked out the moving parts, only to find nothing. Clive tried to restart the beast. No such luck. The engine had seized up. We found out later that a bearing in the alternator had burned out.

We got back on the radio to call Chilo Gorge Lodge. Being down in a hole, as it were, by the river, we couldn't connect with the Lodge directly, or even reach a repeater, for that matter. So we did what any self-respecting traveler would do: We unpacked our picnic and settled down for a festive lunch. I ate half a sandwich and an orange. I figured worse case I could walk the thirty kilometers to the National Parks headquarters at Chipinda Pools in less than eight hours, even though it meant camping out overnight.

What the heck, I thought, *we'll just build a fire late in the afternoon and sleep around it. Not a big deal for an old field geologist.*

After lunch, we decided to get organized. We'd need firewood. But before we began collecting it, we checked our pockets for matches. Would you believe five adults and not a smoker among us? My waterproof match case was at home, naturally, in my Philmont daypack. So much for "Always Prepared." We checked the med kit: No matches. The glove box: No matches. Under the seats: No matches.

Clive lamented, "If only this was a petrol vehicle, not a diesel, we could dip a piece of paper in the fuel tank and then get a spark with the truck battery and start a fire. Too bad, but it can't be done with diesel."

With a stroke of genius, I responded, "Wait a minute! I've got my hand lenses. With the high power lens, I can start a fire on tissue paper."

I proceeded to try this trick for a quarter hour. The winter sun was partly obscured by high thin clouds. There wasn't enough power in the sun's rays to get a rise out of the Kleenex.

Clive announced that he would cross the river and leave a message there for his staff.

"They will drive down the other side and check the spots we had planned to visit. They will leave by 7 p.m. and get to my old camp by nine or ten. If they see a message, they will be here at Fishans by 10 or 11 at night." I looked at him with a whole lot of skepticism.

"Wait a second," I blurted out. "Mike can stay here with Lin and Jackie. I'll walk over to the camp with you." Really, I just didn't want to sit around. I'm not good at it.

Clive and I took off at a wicked pace. For a tree stump of a man, he can really motor! Not more than two hundred meters on, he pulled up short. An enormous Gonarezhou bull elephant was in the grove of trees we were approaching, blocking our path.

"Head over to the cliff, toward the river and go around. I'll walk between you and the bull."

He immediately started making low guttural noises—elephant talk. I stepped off the cliff. I was in alluvial sand of the river valley, so I just walked-slid on down, shook out my Tevas at the bottom, and hoofed as fast as I could to the northeast. After a hundred meters or so, I climbed back up and peeked over the edge. There was Clive walking as fast as he could, the elephant standing right where he had been the last time I looked. I hopped up over the cliff

Gonarezhou elephant that took exception to our disturbing his mud bath, 2006.

and caught up to Clive. It was not easy, I might add. He can really walk damn fast when motivated. But, then again, a Gonarezhou bull nearby would motivate anyone with a brainstem.

"I told the big guy we were okay, and weren't going to bother him."

"Just what I would have said, Clive, if I could talk elephant," I retorted.

We approached a break in the cliff where elephants had trod a path to the river. I had been here before.

"You know, Clive, Russell and I thought about setting up camp right over there, the day before we visited you in 2003." I pointed to a flat spot off to one side. "But we moved over to where we left Lin, Jackie, and Mike, because we spotted an enormous bull. I don't think it was the same one, but Russell thought better of having a Gonarezhou bull stomp down our tent, so we motored over to Fishans. I'd say our tent site ended up about ten meters from where the Land Cruiser died. That's a pretty weird coincidence. I camped out one night in this part of the world and we get stuck thirty feet from the same spot."

"Gonarezhou elephants are pretty aggressive," Clive agreed. "Russell did the right thing, moving your campsite." My opinion of Russell jumped a notch.

We moved through the elephant walk and reached the river. The Runde was very low and wide at this spot—an easy crossing. We took off our sandals and crossed barefoot. I have no idea why, but that's what we did. My Tevas are original "River Guides." Just as good in water as on land. I carried them anyway. Halfway across, I spotted beady little eyes breaking the surface of the river. A crocodile was watching us from a distance of not more that twenty meters. I'd been keeping an eye out since the moment I dipped a toe in the water. The water was only calf deep and cold, so I figured the croc wasn't going to move very fast, or be very interested in a late lunch. Still, I thought it best to move along. We reached the other side a minute later, washed the sand out from between our toes, and put our sandals back on.

"Clive, just when were you going to point out that crocodile watching us in midstream?"

"Oh, you did spot him, did you? Good eyes, Ed."

As we climbed up the far bank and walked along the verge, Clive belatedly explained. "You see, Shangaans never acknowledge the presence of a croc when they are in the water. If you don't name the croc it won't eat you." Clive may look white, but I'm convinced he's as Shangaan as his Mahenya neighbors.

"This area is really dangerous, Ed," Clive started. "Sometimes great herds of Cape buffalo come down to drink. If you see a buffalo, I recommend we jump over the cliff and hoof it over to the river. Also, keep an eye out for lion. There's not a lot of room for us to maneuver between here and the cliff."

Did I mention we didn't have a gun between us? We continued walking at a fast pace and I didn't lag behind. There were scattered great scrubby bushes along the way. I envisioned something unpleasant to be waiting behind each one. No such luck! After another kilometer or so, we arrived at Clive's old camp. All that was left standing was a roundel covered with thatch. Here and there, concrete slabs and scattered building blocks marked where the sleeping chalets once stood. We collected some blocks and propped up the sign Lin had painted on a big sheet of drawing paper:

CHILO

WE ARE BROKEN, TIRED AND COLD.

PLEASE PICK US UP AT FISHANS

LIN & CLIVE.

How dramatic. That's Lin.

The afternoon was wearing on. We didn't dally. An hour later we were back in camp. But not before we happened upon recent spore of both lion and leopard on "our" side of the river. The idea of waiting around without a campfire did not appeal.

"Clive, let's try the petrol trick using diesel. I think I can make up tinder so fine that we can get a fire going," I suggested. Clive agreed to try. He worked on getting to the battery, which for some strange reason was under the front passenger seat. Our radio wires would substitute for jumper cables. We could always reattach the radio wires later. We didn't need a radio just at that moment, we needed a spark!

We hauled mopane logs and branches to the fire pit. As usual, the elephants had supplied us with plenty of firewood. I found a little cup-shaped chunk of mopane. Next to the truck we prepared little piles of very fine kindling, not-so-fine kindling, and small and medium sized sticks. Clive took a long stick, notched the end, put a quarter of a Kleenex in the notch, and shoved it down the fill pipe of the fuel tank. I made a nest of very fine kindling mixed with shredded tissue, stuck in the diesel-wet Kleenex, and wrapped dry grass around it. It resembled a sparrow's nest. I held it next to Clive and the battery. Clive placed the wire ends on top of our masterpiece and sparked. No smoke, no fire. Again, and then again. On the third try I saw a faint green glow. I pulled the "cup" out and blew little puffs on the pile and poof! A teeny flame appeared directly above the diesel-wet Kleenex. The fumes had ignited the shredded Kleenex and grass!

I carried the "cup" a meter from the truck and built a small campfire right on the ground. A couple of minutes later, after it was well established, we transferred the fire to the fire pit. By the time the sun set, around 5:30, we had a bonfire going, wood enough to last two days, and the Land Cruiser seats on the ground for mattresses. We had leftovers for dinner and my hand-crank Brookstone flashlight for anyone who needed to visit a "lava tree" in the night. Earlier that afternoon, Jackie discovered that there were bats living in the bottom of the Fishans outhouse. Someone once told her a story about a guy, a bat, and an outhouse. You get the picture. Nobody used the outhouse.

I fell asleep at about 8 p.m. with Jackie sitting bolt upright alongside me. I don't think she ever closed her eyes. I'm sure it was the beauty of the African night sky, not the thought that lions were going to sneak up on her!

Around 10 p.m., I was rudely awakened by a loud squawk from the radio.

"Alpha One, this is Chilo One. Do you read me?"

A half hour later, two lodge trucks rolled up—a tow truck and a Land Cruiser. A two-hour "mad hatters" ride in the pitch dark, along tracks only a sadomasochist would call a road, and we were back at the lodge. It was 1 a.m. All we wanted was to go to bed. We walked through the main entrance of Chilo Gorge Lodge and there was the majordomo standing along the wall. "Dinner is served," he announced, formally in a deep voice. The whole staff had stayed up to wait on our return. There was nothing to do. We sat down and ate a four-course meal and drank wine until it was appropriate to stagger off to bed.

We drove back to Senuko the next morning. We passed a "vendor" on the roadside selling something charred on the end of sticks.

Jackie enquired of Clive. "Clive, oh Clive, what are they selling? Is it something to eat?"

Clive looked around and up at Jackie. "They're charred mice, dear. Would you like to try one?"

I piped up. "Oh boy, let's stop. Come on, Clive, let's stop."

Clive chose to ignore the little boy sitting next to him.

—

We spent the next couple of quiet days at the lodge. Hunters were at Senuko. Important hunters. Rich American hunters seeking elephant and lion. That's a $50,000 hunt. Jackie and I took our meals with the hunters. I now understand why you can't mix hunters and environmentalists. Big game hunters are really boring people. They talk about their guns. They talk about their ammo. They are about as colorful as a cloudy day. After a couple of days of lackluster repartee, we kept pretty much to ourselves.

I rode my mountain bike most mornings. I had to keep away from the hunters. Not that they would actually shoot me, but they had paid for a bush experience. Having a maniac on a bicycle cross their path probably would not have qualified. Finally the hunters left and we had some time alone before the next group arrived.

Jackie and I took a walk early one morning with Thomas. We left the lodge and walked between the two kopjes that form a kind of entrance to the car park. We headed off northeast around the taller kopje toward a pan that sits on the east side of a sandy vlei. We hadn't gone a quarter of a mile when Thomas stopped me with a hand on my shoulder. There, in front of a patch of low-lying granite boulders, was a black rhino. We were pretty exposed, but there was a little bit of screening thorn bush between us and the bull.

I took Jackie's hand and whispered, "Back up slowly."

I steered us toward the mopane trees just behind us. We positioned ourselves next to a couple of easily climbable trees and waited. We could hear the bull breathing: huff, puff. He walked off around and behind the granite boulders to where we couldn't see him.

"Now what," I whispered to Thomas.

"Stay still for a minute. Then I'll walk on ahead and see where he's gone. I'll wave if it is safe."

We hugged our respective trees while Thomas walked ahead in a semi-crouch. He waved and we walked up the dirt track to where he was standing.

"He's moved off. It's safe for us to walk on. Just keep a climbable tree in sight at all times until I give you the 'all's safe.'"

We continued up the trail toward the water hole. As we passed through an area of patchy small mopane trees (mostly grassy veldt, really) I saw something white maybe twenty-five meters off the trail. We walked over. It was brown hyena poop. The poop of a brown hyena, that is. Hyenas are known as scavengers but, in fact, they hunt small game, like impala. Unlike lions, hyenas tend to leave nothing behind. Their great jaws can crush the bones of just about anything smaller than a giraffe or elephant.

I noticed a slight movement in the grass. There, eating the second pile of hyena poop, was a little leopard tortoise. Thomas grinned. "Nothing is wasted on the Lowveld. This is why you hardly ever see skeletons. The hyena eats the bones. That poop is white from all the calcium. The tortoise needs calcium and eats the poop."

I think Jackie would have brought that little turtle home in her handbag had she been allowed. He was so cute. But that's the trouble with working in conservation. You can't afford to break even the tiniest of rules, let alone import a species banned by the Convention on International Trade in Endangered Species (CITES).

Small leopard tortoise eating hyena poop, SVC, 2004.

The following day, I was out on my bicycle and developed a minor problem with the chain. So, after getting my hands filthy with chain oil and achieving no improvement, I stopped by the workshops and let the mechanic remove, clean, and lube the chain. I'm mechanical enough to clean my hands, and that's about it. It was nearly lunchtime as I got back on my bike and pitched down to the main road. Just before the turn, I spotted a chameleon crossing the dirt road. I picked it up and put it on my shoulder. It clung doggedly to my shirt as I flew down the road back to the lodge. I parked my bike, walked through the lobby area, out past the dining room, and parked the chameleon in a small tree. I went back to our chalet to clean up, dress for lunch, and locate my wife.

About a half hour later, we headed to the outdoor dining area. A family had pitched up for lunch, an unusual occurrence. There was a mom, dad, very well dressed, and two little girls who had already been excused from the table and were running around on the grass between the dining area and the waterhole viewing area—around the tree which, unbeknownst to them, held a beautiful, yellow-green, six-inch-long chameleon.

I walked over, picked the little guy off the tree branch he occupied, and carried him over to the little girls. They were all screams and giggles as I showed them the marvels of the chameleon, talked about its hunting behavior and its independently directed telescope-looking eyeballs. We had migrated back toward the dining area and ended up in front of the little girls' parents, so I showed them the chameleon as well. Clive had come in for lunch by then and stood to the side until I was done.

The family politely finished up, swept up their kids, and left. We sat down to lunch with Clive and Lin. Clive had a very amused look on his face. As the first course arrived, a fruit compote with papaya, apple, and some other tropical fruit, maybe star fruit, Clive said, "Ed that was the governor of Masvingo Province and his family. They are Shona (that is, from the Shona tribe). Do you know what the chameleon represents to the Shona?"

Oh shit, what kind of cultural faux pas have I committed this time? I thought to myself.

Clive grinned wide. "The chameleon is the harbinger of death."

CHAPTER 15

How to Jet-Wash a Rhino

A CALL CAME IN FROM one of the game scouts. A rhino calf had been caught in a wire snare and appeared badly injured. Clive radioed the rhino team. Just a day later, they appeared on the Senuko airstrip. Raoul arrived in his little Husky, and John, Natasha, Chris Foggins (the vet), that is, the rest of the team jumped out of John's Robinson 44 helicopter. Over drinks at the lodge bar we discussed the plan.

The Senuko scouts would locate the rhino mom and calf first thing next morning. Raoul would fly the Husky Graham Connear, the SVC conservator would spot. Once the rhinos were well located, John and Chris would dart the cow from the helicopter, land, and signal for the rest of the team. Clive, Mike Jones, and I decided to drive to the transfer point with the ground team and wait for the helicopter.

Following a quick breakfast of bacon, eggs, baked beans, fried green tomatoes, and rich Zimbabwean coffee, we all took off. The pilots and vet headed for the airstrip and the rest of us piled into a Land Cruiser. Comms squawked back and forth between Raoul and the Senuko scouts. The radio in our Land Cruiser up and died as soon as we got too far from the lodge to turn back. After fussing for a while, Clive found the live radio wire and connected it to the spotlight lead. No kidding. Nothing like improvisation! The spotlight—still attached—got wrapped around the roll bar behind our heads.

As we raced east down the power line road, we spotted three black rhinos, a bull and two full-grown cows, charging through the brush parallel to the road. They finally turned north to get away from us. The Husky, which had previously been flying over us madly waggling its wings in order to direct us while our radio was out, now called down and reported. They had spotted the rhino cow and directed us to a grassy opening alongside the road on which the chopper would land. A few minutes later John and the R-44 arrived. Natasha jumped out of the Land Cruiser and ran over to the chopper. She talked to John for a few seconds and raced back.

"We have a big cow down, but no calf. Seems like Raoul spotted a second cow and mistook it for the mom with the calf. We're going to install a transmitter, so as not to waste our time." She dashed back to the helicopter and jumped in. I expected them to lift off, but John shouted through the open doorway and pantomimed for one of us to hop aboard. Clive, bless his soul, shouted over the blast of the helicopters props, "Ed, go ahead. I'll be able to find you and walk in."

I started to run for the helicopter but stopped abruptly. Twenty-six years ago I had sworn never to fly in a helicopter. My college buddy, Chuck Beverly, had been killed in a helicopter crash in July 1979. If he had called me that day to join him, I would have, but I was with my three-month-old son. When Chuck died, our little group of CSU geology grads took an oath: We would no longer use helicopters in our work. It cost my friend Bill Oriel his job. No matter. Oaths are important.

I yelled back to the vehicle, "Mike, you go with John. I'll walk in with Clive." Mike hoofed it to the helicopter and I rejoined Clive. We walked fast, following the chopper sounds.

Fifteen minutes later we approached the rhino. She looked like an outcropping of gray granite—like part of the landscape. Her head was stuck in the crotch of a thorn tree. Only Chris standing over her gave me an indication of what I was looking at.

Black rhino baby sticking its head in the crotch of a little mopane tree.
Don't know why they do that.

John was circling around, looking for, what I thought at least, was a very small clearing in which to land. He had been in the air looking for a landing zone, or LZ ("el zed" when spoken aloud), while Clive and I were running toward the rhino. Apparently anything reasonably big was too far away from the site, so John put the 'copter down right there. I swear the rotor blades were within a foot of the surrounding mopane trees.

As soon as the props stopped turning the crew hit the ground. I ran up to the helicopter, grabbed a bag, and followed Natasha. As I ran through some knee-high buff-colored grass, I stepped right through a little wait-a-bit thorn. It grabbed around my ankle and sliced a perfect four-inch, razor-thin gash across my lower calf. Unfazed, I ran the last twenty meters to the rhino. John dropped the portable generator and dragged out the chain saw. As he cut out the branches of the thorn bush, Natasha and I pulled them away from the rhino's head. I looked down at my leg, saw the blood, and swiped across the cut with a not-so-clean finger. In the warm, dry air it clotted immediately. John kept sawing and Natasha and I kept hauling away at the branches as they were cut. As soon as we had her head clear of the thorn tree, and with the help of the scouts, we rocked her out and arranged her legs to make her more comfortable. For some unfathomable reason, black rhinos tend to end their drugged run with their head stuck in the crotch of a tree. Go figure!

Chris started drilling at the base of her big horn with what I swear looked like a router. Rhino horn confetti flew everywhere. Once the hole was large enough to take the transmitter, he changed drill bits and put on the longest, biggest bit I have ever seen. It must have been more than a foot and a half long. John clipped the end of the horn off with the chain saw and Chris steadied the drill bit directly over the center of the horn. Long, spiral streamers of rhino horn whipped out and around the bit. Every few inches, Chris had to stop and we helped unwind and strip off

Black rhino cow: Chris Foggins drilling straight down the horn to implant a transmitter and antenna.

How to jet wash a rhino: Ed, Chris, and Tasha.

the white shavings. All this time, Natasha was monitoring the rhino's blood oxygen level and I counted respirations. Once in a while she walked behind the rhino, lifted her tail, and checked her temperature.

Natasha yelled, "Ed, grab the pump sprayer. She's getting too warm."

The sprayer was a manual thing about two and a half feet tall with a yellow jug, a red screw top, and a black pump handle. Operation was pretty simple: pump, pump, pump, spray.

"Under her belly, then up and down her back," Natasha instructed me in the technique for jet-washing a rhino. One of the scouts started placing mopane branches on her back to give her a little shade. Pump, pump, pump, spray. Repeat.

The transmitter antenna was threaded up through the drill hole, the transmitter was set into the routed hole at the base of the horn, and the whole shebang was epoxied in place. An insulating wrap of ice was placed around the horn to set the epoxy. Ten minutes later Chris told us to leave. We hauled the gear back to the chopper. He gave the reversal drug and he and Natasha climbed conveniently close mopane trees. Clive and I took off running toward the Land Cruiser.

—

Thirty minutes later, the Senuko scouts located mom and baby. We did the whole routine over again. This time Chris darted the right cow. Once again we charged in, but this time, the rest of the crew ran off to catch the baby as soon as Chris had stabilized the mom. Natasha and I were left alone with 3,100 pounds of snoozing rhino. She took charge.

"Call out the respiration rate every minute or so. I'll watch her vital signs."

As she read the thermometer, she said, "She's going to get too warm. Grab the pump and wet her down."

Apparently I'd become the resident power-washer. Pump, pump, pump, spray. Pump, pump, pump, spray. Pump, pump, pump, spray.

"More water, Ed. Gotta keep her wet."

Pump, pump, pump, spray. Pump, pump, pump, spray. Pump, pump, pump, spray.

"Respiration twelve," I called out.

After about ten minutes on our own, John arrived with the equipment and half the team.

Natasha looked at me. "Ed, if you have the stomach for it, why don't you watch Chris and Raoul operate on the calf."

"Where are they?"

"Just about five hundred meters that way," John responded. He pointed back toward the road. "They're in an open grassy area on the other side of the road. You can't miss it."

I wasn't about to explain that I was capable of getting lost in my own house. Instead, I thanked Natasha and hoofed it five hundred meters thataway.

Don't think about all the things that you could run into by accident, I said to myself. But of course, I did. *Lions, leopards, mambas, and of course stray rhinos.* Pause. *I said, don't think about it, stupid.*

I spotted the crew standing over a pathetic looking, thirteen-month-old female rhino calf. Her left, rear leg was swollen to twice its normal size. The rest of her was skin and bones. The huge festering wound was crawling with maggots. Chris and Raoul discussed the problem. Raoul outlined a scar higher up her leg with his finger. His fingernail snapped over what looked like a thorn stuck in

Baby black rhino foot caught in copper snare. Note the scar above the festering wound. That snare was removed from around the bone.

her tough hide. On closer inspection, I could see the tip of two wires. A second snare was almost completely under healed skin, most of it right up against the bone. Only the twisted end of the snare was still visible. They would have to operate and remove both snares.

"What can I do, guys?" I asked.

"Care to hand us instruments, Ed?"

"Sure," I said out loud.

Then I had a little private conversation with my innards: *You will not embarrass me in front of these people,* I demanded.

Chris turned to Mike. "How about calling out respiration?"

We got to work. The operation took place on a sheet of rubber matting. Chris injected the baby with penicillin and stuck a hypodermic of reversal drug in her ear—ready to use in case she went into respiratory failure, the usual cause of the loss of a drugged animal.

We discussed the procedure. "As you can see by the twisted wire, the snare is under the skin, maybe all the way up against the bone. The best way to remove it will be to find the snare on the opposite side of her leg, cut the wire and pull it through on this side."

Operating gear. Both copper and iron fence wire snares are visible. Observe orange handled wire cutters.

Raoul proceeded to make an incision where he expected to find the wire. He cut parallel to the scar and cut deeply. The rhino's blood was dark red and quickly clotted into jellylike globs. With the scalpel he felt around for the wire. He snapped it with the point of the scalpel.

"Ed, hand me the wire cutters."

I got the picture, and it was not going to be pretty. Raoul shoved the nose of the wire cutters into the open wound until he could grip the wire. After working it around for a minute or two, he snipped it with the wire cutters.

"Let me have the needle-nose pliers, now."

I looked around. The operating theatre resembled an auto mechanic's toolbox. I handed him the pliers. Using the pliers and wire cutters he untwisted the wires at the back of the rhino's leg, pulled them apart and with a struggle, pulled one-half of the wire cleanly out of the calf's leg. He tried to repeat the performance with the other half, but it wouldn't give. He tugged again. Once more it didn't move. Finally, he put a foot on the rhino's leg and pulled for all he was worth. The wire snare was doubled up on one side. It came away with blood and tissue attached. My stomach gave a little lurch. That was pretty gruesome, but at least we had the wire snare out. I looked it over. It was standard iron fence wire—the kind that was used in the conservancy perimeter fence that was being dismantled by poachers.

We went to work on the second wire. This one was truly disgusting.

As I mentioned, the largest open wound was full of maggots that had to be cleaned out. Certain fly maggots are actually beneficial in an open wound. They clean out rotten flesh and leave healthy tissue behind. Not in this case. These were screwworm maggots. We cleaned them out with our fingers and managed to expose the wire in the open wound.

I immediately grasped why this wound was so much worse. The snare was made from copper telephone wire. The copper probably contributed to the lack of healing we observed. "Copper," Chris observed, "is poisonous."

Raoul made an incision on the front side of the calf's leg, just like the last one. In the background Mike continued calling out respiration rate. We all looked at him and Chris at once. The last rate Mike had called out was "thirty." Two breaths a minute! The calf was going into respiratory failure. We waited. Mike called out "fifty-five." One breath per minute. Chris reached in his bag and pulled out a length of rope. He tied it loosely around the rhino's front legs. He looked across at us and said quietly, "Everyone have a tree?"

He was about to give the calf the reversal drug. If it got too much it could jump up and trample somebody. The first rule of rhino work is *have a tree to climb*. I looked around and found something I could climb. Chris pressed the hypo plunger. "Six." "Fifteen," Mike called out. The rhino lifted its head just a little and settled back down. "Twelve!" The little rhino's breathing had stabilized at about 6 breaths per minute. Chris had given her just enough of the drug but not too much. After forty years of this work I suppose Chris knows what he's up to. We went back to operating. When Raoul went in with the wire cutters the little rhino flinched. She could feel the pain. So could I. But in the end we got the copper wire out. Large doses of screw worm powder, purple antiseptic all over the place, another large dose of penicillin in the butt end and voila! We were done. Everything was picked up and we retreated to the vehicles. Chris delivered the rest of the reversal drug and three minutes later the little girl struggled to her feet.

"Chris, what are the odds on her surviving the wound and operation and all."

"Well, Ed, I'd give her not more than one-in-three. If she finds her mum, and her mum sticks with her, and she stays on her feet for the first three days, well then I reckon that she's going to make it."

Three days later, as we were packing the truck to catch the Sugar Cane flight to Harare, the scouts reported they had a visual on the calf and she was limping alongside her mom. I've had two subsequent reports from Raoul a couple of months apart. She was completely healed and walking normally. She will stay with her mom for another year and a half until she's about three years old. I expect to meet her someday, while walking or biking on Senuko ranch. I'd like to see them together before they split up. And, I shall. Mom has a working transmitter in her nose. And me, I have a bike waiting for me at Senuko Ranch.

CHAPTER 16

Hallucinating a
Peace Parks Meeting

IN 2006, WE ARRIVED IN Harare to attend a series of meetings. Once again, we stayed with Mary Ann. She was renting out a couple of her rooms to transient whites who were on their way out of the country. Mugabe's "indigenization" policies were having their intended effect: drive the remaining whites out of the country.

If you believe that blacks can't be racist, you haven't lived in Zim. Mind you, it's not the regular people—it's the political fat cats. They use race as a political tool. They use it crudely and stupidly. After a while, you hope that it's a sign that race is the last tool of a failed politic, but no, Mugabe and his thugs are still around, wandering the path of destruction they have been carving for decades. I'm afraid that black Zimbabweans are not like Americans or Libyans, Egyptians, or Nicaraguans. The average Zim would rather starve under a despot than raise his head above the trench and risk it being shot off.

One of the fleeing families left a car behind. Mike was using it as his "around town" transport. There were no papers with it, so he had to navigate around police roadblocks. I saw a lot of Harare's back streets on that trip.

Jackie, Mary Ann, and I started planning one of our epic parties. We decided to hold it after our return from the Lowveld.

—

We spent the better part of a week relaxing at Senuko Lodge and traveling around the bush with Lin and Clive. Some days Clive and I checked out local geology. Clive had worked for a mining company right out of university. He loves geology almost as much as me.

One day we scoped out a perfectly circular geological feature.

"Say, Ed," Clive had asked. "Do you think that's a meteorite crater?"

I checked out an old Rhodesian Geological Survey map of the area. The hill had been mapped as a "ring dike," a geological structure usually associated with a volcanic neck.

"Let's check it out," I said. "Maybe the RGS got it wrong."

Off we went to the southeast corner of his neighbor's Chigwete Ranch, between Senuko and the Turgwe River.

We drove to the base of the hill through dun-colored grass. The hill was steep, but I wanted to walk up through the structure. Geologists tend to avoid trails, unless they are fresh road cuts. We like to cut our own paths over geological structures and then reverse and walk parallel to them, effectively creating a geological map—in this case, in my head.

We climbed up a series of small cliffs composed of more or less flat lying sediments. I beat the rocks with my hammer. Through my hand lens, I could see rounded grains of quartz.

"This must be lower Karoo. The outcrop is composed of coarse sand and grit."

We climbed higher, watching out for mambas and other small annoyances.

We crested the top of the last sandstone cliff and voila! We were standing on a vertically emplaced band of glassy black rock.

"Hey, Clive. This is glassy basalt or peridotite! This thing really is volcanic!"

The RGS had got it right. We crossed into a central depression in the hill. There were maybe five or ten acres of beautifully forested savanna and grassland right in the center of this volcanic neck.

"Clive, this is the most beautiful site for a safari lodge I've ever seen. It's like we're in a park."

We walked along and spotted a break in the outside wall of the ring dike. Naturally, an intermittent stream had cut a drainage path out of the central "crater."

I stumbled on a boulder, unseen in the grass. When I picked it up, I grinned. "Look at this, Clive. Coarse grained, nearly black peridotite, mostly orthopyroxene. This volcanic neck is second cousin to a diamond pipe."

Clive looked at me. "De Beers [the diamond giant] has been all through this area. If there were a diamond pipe we'd know about it by now." I didn't contradict him, but actually, he was wrong: De Beers would have kept it secret. You see, diamonds aren't rare. In fact, they're common. The reason they are so expensive is the best monopoly and marketing the world has ever seen. De Beers has way too many diamonds, thus they would never have mined this site.

We found a game trail and headed through the narrow defile formed by a stream to exit the "crater." As we rounded a corner we walked into a humongous cloud of dust. We heard a series of snorts, followed immediately by crashing through the trees below us. We looked at each other. Clive walked on a few paces.

"Look at the print on the trail, Ed. Can you see the skin print in the dust?"

It was clear as can be.

"That's the print of a black rhino bull. He was sleeping right here on this path. He could have just as easily charged right through us."

I looked at the defile behind us. There was nowhere we could have run.

Back at camp, I picked a dozen so-called black pepper ticks off me. I crossed my fingers I wouldn't get tick fever from the tiny buggers.

—

Three days later, Jackie and I were considering a nap after lunch, but I was feeling restless. Clive and Lin had left the lodge and returned to their home about five kilometers away. "I'm going for a walk," I announced to Jackie. She looked at me strangely. I took off down a dirt track. She ran up to the office and found Thomas, the lodge's head guide. About five minutes later, they caught up with me.

"What are you doing, Ed?" Thomas asked. "You shouldn't be out walking without a gun."

I grinned at him. "Oh, don't worry. Nothing's going to eat me."

Thomas and Jackie walked along. After a half hour I was getting a little light-headed.

"Let's head back, I think I need a laydown," I said.

A couple of hours later, I dismissed the staff. They weren't going to serve us dinner, so they might as well go home. The only person left was the security guard, a Shangaan who spoke nary a word of English.

Two hours later, as the sun was setting, a violent thunderstorm rolled over the savanna and lightning flashed brilliantly very close by. The thunder was fantastic. I lay under the mosquito net thinking, *If I'm hallucinating, I really like it. The colors, the sounds—wow!*

I was running a 104-degree fever.

At eight o'clock Clive and Lin arrived at our chalet. What they saw when they walked in, as they described it later, was like a movie.

"There was Jackie surrounded by candles (she had robbed the other chalets), lightning flashing overhead, lions roaring not a hundred meters away, and she's sitting quietly reading a story to Ed. You were thrashing and talking irrationally. She was sitting there totally calm."

"He came down with this fever. No one was here, so I've just been reading to him."

Clive "interviewed" me. He went into my medical kit and pulled out the Artemether.

"You don't have a malarial headache, but the other symptoms are suspect. Swallow this and take the whole course."

As it turned out, I didn't have malaria. I didn't even have tick fever. But taking the malaria drug was the right thing to do. Artemether has no side effects. It can't hurt, even if you don't have the real thing.

The next day, I broke out with a hemorrhagic rash on my chest, arms, and legs. My joints felt funny. I tried closing my fist. *Uh, uh.* I tried bending my wrist, then an ankle. The fever had attacked my joints.

I picked up pencil and paper and began a journal, recording the course of my illness. The following day, the fever broke, more or less.

We were supposed to go to a Peace Parks meeting at the Hakamela Education Center on Malilangwe Conservancy about one and a half hours away.

"Ordinarily, I wouldn't recommend you go to the meeting, Ed, but the chairman of Malilangwe is Colin Saunders, my doctor. I think he should look at you."

Two hours later, the meeting convened. Clive didn't even have to ask Colin. He took one look at me, did a double take, and called over one of his boys.

"Prepare chalet 16, please, Trust." Turning back to me, he said, "I want you to go with Trust and lay down. At the first break [for tea, of course], I will give you a physical exam. You probably have tick fever, but I'm not sure."

As promised, Colin came by at teatime. I stripped naked and he examined every square inch of my body—every crack and crevasse, as it were.

Exam over, he scratched his head. "You don't have the telltale bull's-eye from a tick bite. The last time I saw anything like this was thirty years ago. I think you have chikungunya virus. It's a mosquito-transmitted arbovirus common to Mauritius and India. How you got it is a mystery! I'll check with a virologist friend of mine in South Africa and let you know what he thinks. In the meantime, don't worry. It isn't fatal. You will just be crippled with arthritis for the next six months and then the symptoms will fade away."

That was encouraging. And, it explained why I couldn't close my fist.

Two days later, we returned to Harare and threw our garden party. Among the guests was Roan Martin, possibly the leading expert on elephants worldwide. I wore bush shorts, naturally, which invited comments on the big splotches of pink skin decorating my arms and legs from a group of veterinarians, one of whom was my friend, Chris Foggins.

He looked me over and said, "So, Ed, have you ever heard of 'Crimean-Congo Hemorrhagic Fever?'"

"No, Chris. What about it?"

"Well," grinning at his vet friends, "it looks just like that—pointing first at my arm and then at my leg. If that's what you have, well, I suppose you're dead by now."

"Let me get you all some beer. You clearly aren't drinking enough," I said as I walked away.

When I got back to the States later that week, I had my blood drawn at a lab, placed the vials on ice in a cooler bag, and drove it up to the Foothills Campus of Colorado State University. Dr. Terry White of the CDC (Centers for Disease Control) had agreed to test my blood.

I was hoping for a tour of their Level 3 lab. Level 4 is where they test for Ebola and other deadly bugs. Level 3 is "contagious, but not fatal."

I drove up to the gate and to my surprise was met by three marine guards, two with AR-15s. "Please open your trunk and hood." I popped the switches. They searched my engine block, then the trunk, and then ran mirrors under the chassis.

As I waited, a lab assistant sped down the hill in a golf cart. "Sorry, the lab is restricted."

I handed her the blood samples and three pages of typewritten text.

"Please give these to Terry. During and immediately after my illness, I wrote down a layman's description of the course of the disease. I think she might find it interesting."

Up the hill she went. I drove home, trying to recover from my astonishment.

They're studying a flu bug. Armed guards? For god's sake!

Two weeks later, Terry called me.

"Hi, Ed, we got the results back. You definitely had chikungunya, an arbovirus and second cousin to West Nile. We tested you for other viruses and parasites. You're completely clean, otherwise."

She paused. "By the way, I showed your three-page write-up to my colleagues. We all agree: We've never seen such an accurate description from a layperson. We'd like to publish it. Would that be okay with you?"

"Sure," I responded, and then promptly forgot about it.

About a year later, I was cleaning up some files and came across the pdf file of my blood tests.

Hmmm, I thought, *I wonder if they ever published the paper.*

So, I Googled it. Here's what came up: Warner, E., et al, "Chikungunya Reported among International Travelers, 2005–2006," in *CDC MMWR Weekly*, September, 29, 2006/55(38); 1040–1042.

I've published a virology paper. They had even made me "first author." There's immortality for you.

CHAPTER 17

My Olympian Caretaker

WE HEADED BACK TO ZIM in August 2007 to visit the Save Valley Conservancy. I was anticipating two weeks of Rhino Ops with the crew pitching up at Senuko Ranch in about five days.

The Lodge on Senuko Ranch sits atop a granite kopje, one of the small hills that poke their nose out of the flat sand washes of the southeast Lowveld.

Jackie and I settled into chalet 3, our favorite. Just below the open porch was a large flat slab of rock sloping down toward the water hole. At night we could hear and dimly see everything going on below us.

The Senuko chalets have thatched roofs and are open on three sides. Green khaki tent material can be unrolled at night, but it's really rare for mambas or lions to climb in with you so we usually leave them open.

August is winter on the Lowveld and it can get really cold. Once in a while a Guti blows in from the Cape bringing drizzle, fog, and damp cold. On those nights, the staff will put a hot water bottle in the bottom of your bed. It can be surprising if you're not expecting it. Years earlier as safari tourists we heard an American woman scream in terror when she crawled into bed. False alarm! It was not an animal, just a hot water bottle.

Our first evening at the lodge, Clive explained to us that he had a little job to do before Rhino Ops commenced.

"I've been invited by the Mahenya community to give a talk at the twenty-fifth anniversary of the formation of the provincial government."

"You mean the celebration is in Mozambique?" I asked. The Mahenya community extends across the border into Mozambique.

Chalet #3, Senuko Lodge, SVC, where I usually lived when working at the conservancy, 2004.

"Sure. Do you want to come? We'll cross the Runde River in a Land Cruiser, pick up the dirt track, and drive down to Massanenga. It's only about fifty miles from here. Doesn't take more than about three hours."

"What about the border?"

"Leave your passports here. You will be guests of the government," he replied.

—

We drove to the Mahenya community on the Zimbabwean side of the border with a second Land Cruiser, picked up Chief Mahenya and his entourage, and loaded them into the other vehicle. We then attached a trailer to our truck and loaded up the village football team.

That's right, we forded the Runde River with a high school football team in tow. We drove across country and intercepted a real road (i.e., a much improved four-wheel-drive dirt track) that took us to the outskirts of Massanenga. We dropped the tow at the soccer stadium.

After we were introduced to the local dignitaries, I walked around. I can't help it; I go into meet-and-greet mode wherever I go. The only reason I haven't gone into politics is that I refuse to demean myself.

I noticed a group of whites hanging around their camper on the east side of the soccer field. They hadn't approached the bandstand where we "dignitaries" were directed to sit during the speeches and entertainment. As I approached I could hear them talking. It was clear that they were South African professional hunters and their wives. The women's faces were covered with so much makeup you'd have thought they had been through an outbreak of smallpox.

I had heard stories of less-than-ethical South African hunters coming into Mozambique to hunt on communal areas. Maybe these were some of them. They seemed to be shunned by the locals. I walked away.

The speeches commenced. We were the only whites in a sea of black men wearing dark suits (with the little label still on the sleeve so you'd know they were designer clothes) and black women dressed magnificently in their colorful prints. We four, dressed in khaki, stood out, to say the least.

The speeches were given in Portuguese. Oh my aching head! The dancing and singing, on the other hand, were marvelous.

The performances wrapped up after a couple of hours. Clive informed us that we were invited to the private luncheon. We drove off into the bush a couple of kilometers. There, in a clearing, were tables set up and around the corner, slap-together bleachers, and a speaker's platform. The politicians got up and delivered another load of talks in Portuguese. I went into my happy place—you know, the place where nothing intrudes on you, even in the most unpleasant of situations.

Clive gave a speech in Shangaan, not Portuguese. The crowd of onlookers went wild. He was speaking their native tongue. I couldn't understand a word, but I could see how the atmosphere had changed.

The lunch was fascinating. Every couple of places, there was a setup of Fanta soft drink, beer, and an execrable Portuguese wine. Great pots and plates of food arrived. The meat dishes were either grilled or boiled. The preferred approach to butchering meat is to chop it with an axe, basically ignoring the animal's anatomy. Chicken, goat, and mombie were all chopped up in much the same style. I ate and drank so much that I actually grew to like the Portuguese wine. I liked it so much that I insisted we buy a case before we departed. When I tried to drink a bottle a week later, I almost gagged.

Astrid

We drove back to Senuko the next day, the Land Cruiser loaded with sacks of maize and wheat flour, tins of cooking oil and, of course, the case of wine. Staples were not available in the collapsing Zimbabwe economy.

When we got back, the rhino team had already arrived and was organizing. That evening at dinner I met the new girl in town, Astrid Huelin, a British veterinarian.

Raoul had informed me that I would be working with Astrid, but I was impressed to meet another six-foot, blonde goddess. Naturally curly, golden-blonde hair framed her round face and widely spaced blue eyes.

Really? What do they feed them when they are babies?

That night I woke up around 1 a.m. with the worst case of food poisoning I'd ever had. I was so sick I was in the loo most of the night. Even so, I kept thinking about the poor bats that lived in the roof of our bathroom and how I was ruining their lives.

The next morning, we all met for breakfast. I was white as a sheet. The team was solicitous. "Sick drunk again, huh, Ed. It'll be 110 degrees today. You're gonna die."

"I'll be just fine, goddamnit. I waited a whole year for this. I'm not going to miss it just because I'm half dead from puking my guts out."

We drove off looking for a black rhino that needed to be dehorned. We drove around for about an hour trying to follow the information we were receiving from the scouts about where the rhino was headed. Finally we stopped at a water hole.

Astrid got out of the vehicle. "Ed, I'm exhausted. Let's take a nap under that acacia." We lay down in the dust next to each other. I passed out.

All day long, Astrid was solicitous of me. It was wonderful. I was so fucked up that it never occurred to me that she was just mothering me—probably because Raoul had told her I was a donor.

As usual, I recovered really fast. I was running through the thorn bush like my normal maniacal self the next day.

Our routine each day was the same. Get up early. Drive like crazy. Run through the bush carrying chainsaws, medical supplies, and water sprayers. Chase drugged rhino hoping that we wouldn't catch up to it too soon or too late.

Dehorning, in which the horn is cut off about two inches above the growing base and then trimmed so that it isn't left squared off, is done with a chainsaw. The horn and trimmings are always turned over to a National Parks representative. Every year, CITES inspects the vaults to make sure no one is poaching the horn from inside the government.

Every evening we'd drive back to camp sometime between 5 and 10 p.m. We'd clean up, dress for dinner, hit the bar, and hope not to fall down the hill between the bar and the dining room after drinking on an empty stomach. My "boss" would hit her chalet, her overalls covered in dust, poop, and blood. A half hour later she would emerge with her blonde hair spiked with gel, wearing a sari. Amazing!

I would wait for Astri (no longer Astrid) at the foot of the path leading to the bar. We'd walk up the steps most of the way holding hands. I'd hop up a couple of steps ahead of her and give her a peck on the lips. The gang would hoot and holler. Well, everyone except my wife. She'd just stare. Jackie is a really good sport. She knew where I'd be spending the night. It wasn't with Astri.

Sometime during the first week, I mentioned to John, my trusty helicopter pilot and good buddy, about how Astri had mothered me that first day. He just grinned.

"Ed, you don't know about Astrid?" I waited for the story to come.

"Astrid was on the British Olympic Team. She rowed single oar. That girl is the strongest, toughest woman I know. I was helping Chris teach the 'Dangerous Drugs' course when she attended. You've heard that it gets a little wild, especially after grades. The last night is usually a complete drunken brawl. Nobody who was there will ever forget two of the vets going after Astrid. They had been rugby players in their youth. Before they knew what hit them she had both in headlocks at the same time—one under each armpit. They had to cry uncle. Otherwise she'd have killed them. I'm telling you, that is one tough cookie."

I looked across the bar with a newfound respect.

"I think she likes you, you old goat."

—

The next day, our task was to pick up a wandering black rhino bull.

Save Valley Conservancy was being invaded by indigenous farmers from the Gudu community on the east side of the Save River. They wouldn't touch Clive's ranch because he was a member of the Mahenya community. As I've mentioned, Shangaans considered him as one of them, therefore other local black communities respect him greatly. Regardless, they were only a few miles from his east and north borders, having invaded the abandoned Levanga Ranch and the Humani Ranch, owned by a truly obnoxious white Zimbo named Roger Whittle. It was estimated that there were more than three thousand "invaders" in that area of the conservancy—maybe ten thousand in all on about 300,000 acres.

On the east side of the Save Valley Conservancy, Levanga is tucked up between the Save River and Clive's ranch, Senuko. It is another thirty-thousand-acre plot derived from the original Devuli Ranch. Across the river, the Gudu community has invaded Levanga. They didn't actually drive off the white owners since they never lived on Levanga. I believe that during the bad times the two brothers moved from Harare to New Zealand. Clive had entered into a long-term lease with an option to purchase Levanga, but somehow, typical of Clive (who is a world-class conservationist, but also, possibly the worst businessman I ever partnered with), the lease agreement was never signed. Nonetheless, Clive took care of the property and used the hunting quota as if it were his own.

Levanga ranch house was composed of three or four buildings and an airstrip. After twenty years of disuse the buildings were all overgrown, roofs caved in and vines growing in the cracks in the concrete and cinder block. Rhino Ops sometimes used the Levanga airstrip and camped in or around the buildings. A Sabi Star, one of the more startling indigenous plants of the southeast Lowveld, grows in front of the main gate. The first time I drove up to Levanga, sitting next to Natasha in a borrowed Land Cruiser, I was happily amazed at what I saw. Also known as the desert rose, or mock azalea, the Sabi Star is a succulent or cactus in the dogbane family. Bare gray, sticklike branches end with five-pointed pink or pink and white flowers about an inch across when it is in bloom in the winter. The white sap is used to tip poison arrows. The Sabi Star grows wild in south and east Africa and the Arabian Peninsula. Its name comes from the Save or Sabi River.

—

The bull had crossed the Turgwe River heading south and east. The countryside was mopane forest and acacia scrub, but areas had been burned and planted with maize by the invaders who cared little that the Lowveld cannot sustain subsistence farming due to low and unpredictable rainfall. In nine years they only successfully harvested one crop of maize and a small crop of sorghum. Most of the farmers had huts on these fields; some had second wives living in those huts, but most of the invaders still lived across the Save River in the Gudu community. Nonetheless, this rhino was going to get poached if we didn't get him out of harm's way.

It took the better part of two days to locate him. He was pretty good at hiding in the acacia scrub, looking like an outcrop of Karoo basalt. It was midafternoon when we finally ran him to ground. Fortunately, the area has decent roads built during the cattle days, so the ground team and the transport lorry were able to get right into the spot where the rhino went down.

This was the most dangerous of Rhino Ops I took part in. This bull was truly massive—well over 3,500 pounds. He also had a pretty serious horn, more than thirty inches long. Getting him into the container would require the skill of the entire team.

Two scout teams arrived, bringing our headcount to about a dozen guys to haul on the front rope that leads through the container and the bolt-hole in the front. Before we got him reversed, we rocked him back and forth until his legs were folded under him in a way that would make it more likely he would stand up in front of the container. The container had been carefully lowered while we held his gigantic head off the ground. We then rested the leading edge of his head on the lip of the container.

"Team ready?" enquired Chris Foggins, to multiple shouts of "yes" in response. He injected the reversal drug and the rhino began to struggle to its feet. We pushed and pulled with all our might. As his head started swinging right and left, we eased up on our effort. He let out a long whoosh of a breath and raised his head. Once again we pushed and pulled. He staggered forward a step. His head was half in the container. The moment of truth was upon us. He was really waking up. Chris whacked him on the ass with the flat of an axe. Two more steps . . . almost in. With another sigh, he cleared the back of the container. I jumped to the left-hand door and John to the right. We closed him in and dropped the latch.

By the time we were ready to transport, the sun had set and the black African night was upon us. That night was partly cloudy with a new moon, and it was extraordinarily dark. Chris had given the rhino a different tranquilizer for the drive.

The trucks moved out. I rode in a Land Cruiser behind the transport truck. Chris was on top of the container, just in case. After half an hour we hit the main conservancy road and took it north about fifteen miles to the northern boma. About halfway there, the container started rocking from side to side. The lorry slid to a stop. Chris reached down into the container, hanging onto a strut with his legs, grabbed the rhino's right ear and pumped another dose of tranquilizer into him. First time I'd seen that!

By the time the transport turned west onto the boma road, we were a couple of minutes behind. As we slowed down and approached the turning I happened to be looking left into the trees. There, walking along, were two lionesses out hunting. We slowed to a stop and watched them turn left and walk parallel to the boma road. Within a few minutes they were going to be up the ass-end of the translocation operation. Clive drove slowly along, keeping them in sight. They angled away to the southwest and we lost sight of them. We climbed out of the vehicle and went to work. Never said a word about the lionesses until we were well into the scotch.

Delivering white rhino to boma on SVC at night, 2009.

The translocation operation really did seem like a cross between *Jurassic Park* and *King Kong*. The scouts were on top of the wooden boma pulling up the twelve-foot long logs that formed the fence of the enclosure.

We had to remove eight of them so that the container could be placed right in the opening. The container was painted white. The lights of the vehicles were on, but most of the lighting was coming from personal headlamps that had appeared out of nowhere for the operation.

I climbed up on top of the container as soon as it was in place. The next step was to open the doors and get out of the way. The rhino was very sleepy but very restless as well. A thump shook the container. Chris hit his shoulder with a cattle prod and he backed partway out. He was waking up. He was smelling humans and he didn't like it. He stepped back into the container and charged the front end with his horn. It was like being in a moderate earthquake! I almost flipped off the top of the container. Chris whacked him a second time and we started yelling at him. He snorted and backed all the way out. The container doors were swung closed and the scouts hurriedly maneuvered the wooden posts back into their slots while the rhino charged into the rear wall a couple of times.

Thank you, lions, for being so considerate and not eating any of us, resounded inside my head.

We didn't get back to Senuko Lodge that night until 10 p.m. As exhausted as everyone was, the routine didn't change. We showered, hit the bar for a whisky, and went to dinner just before midnight.

Fortunately, this was the last exercise of the rhino operation. We could all sleep in until 6:30 before beginning the job of packing everything up.

About two months after returning home, I got email from Clive. The big bull had recrossed the Turgwe River and was back on Levanga, right where we had picked him up.

CHAPTER 18

To Hell with Oaths

I'VE HAD A FEW MISADVENTURES flying in helicopters, including in Alaska and the Gulf of Mexico. In my youth, I probably flew more than 250 bush flights in Hillers, Bells, Jet Rangers, Chinooks, Super Cubs, Beavers, Gooses (not Geese!), and a variety of Cessnas, many of them on floats. In the summer of 1968, I worked the lower Alexander Archipelago for Humble Minerals. I crashed twice, both times in Hillers, and walked away.

Oaths

In 1979, my college buddy, Chuck Beverly, flew to a mineral prospect site in the Red Desert Basin of Wyoming, I would have jumped at the opportunity to go with him—three-month-old son not withstanding—had he invited me. That summer day, the tail rotor assembly on the Bell GB-3 disintegrated, killing Chuck and the pilot. The third seat was empty. Several of my college friends, like Bill Oriel at his gold prospecting business in Nevada, were still using helicopters for their work. Following Chuck's death, we all swore an oath never to fly in helicopters again.

I honored that oath for a long time—right up until July 2005, when

John and Natasha of the rhino team waved me over to the Robinson 44 they were in. I jumped into the empty rear seat and tried to ignore the queer feeling in my gut from breaking the oath. After all, my kid was grown. I'd taken care of my estate. My wife would surely find a well-endowed pool boy to keep her company. Why not take a risk like flying in helicopters? Little did I know, I'd have to think long and hard about that question.

I had flown to Lusaka, Zambia, in 2004 to join Mike Jones on another of our project scouting trips. The plan was to meet up with a couple of Zambians, Darrell and his son, Charles, and fly into a very small and poorly maintained airstrip in West Lunga in northwestern Zambia. As soon as I arrived in Lusaka, I got a call from Mike.

"Cheers, Ed. I'm being rolled into X-ray as we speak. I'm afraid I won't be making it to Zambia. Why don't you go on ahead and visit with Darrell Rea and then come over to Harare. There will be plenty of work here."

"What the hell's wrong, Mike?"

"Don't know, but it hurts like hell in my innards."

Mike had a herniated diaphragm. It was probably a residual consequence of his stepping on a land mine in 1975, the one that blew his leg off.

So, I met Darrell and Charles the next day and arranged to return next year. I flew to Harare shortly thereafter.

If you're wondering why I've bothered telling you this, it is necessary background to the rest of this story. You see, Mike tried to arrange for the flight into West Lunga during my 2005 stay. As it turned out, the mining company donating the airtime was supposed to supply the airplane while I was in Zim. As it happened, the airplane, a Cessna 170, wouldn't become available until after I was scheduled to return to Colorado. Here again is an example of the unintended consequences of timing and luck.

As context for this amazing story, I want to tell you about a previous and parallel experience that happened to me in 1974 on the North Slope of Alaska. In June of that year, I was sent by Amoco Production

Company to supervise the geology on a wildcat well being drilled sixty-eight miles south of Deadhorse, Alaska, the "destination" for Prudhoe Bay Oil Field, then in development. The North Slope, that is, the area between the Chukchi Sea and the Brooks Mountain Range, is the most remote area of the continental United States.

The site consisted of a gravel airstrip just long enough to handle large aircraft like the Hercules, a supply pad, and a drilling location. Connected to the enormous rig was a camp of mobile trailers. Every bit of equipment that was there, including a grader and a pickup truck, had been flown in. The gravel for the strip and pads had been dredged out of the Sagavanirktok River located a half mile from the far end of the airstrip.

My job for six weeks was to examine the little rock chip samples ground up by the drill bit at the bottom of the wellbore and describe them. At that time, the only "mobile" telephone was the RCA satellite phone located in Deadhorse.

My supervisors in Denver demanded a report by phone accompanied by a fax every single day from a little portable unit with which they had supplied me.

Being a little far to walk, I had to use the standby twin-engine Merlin aircraft, which was, under other circumstances, the medical emergency evacuation plane.

The demands of my job and the "normal" use of the aircraft combined with the split authority over the operation created a terrific conflict. You see, Denver told me what to do, but Anchorage—the drilling headquarters for this well—believed that they had absolute control over what happened on location. It was a great big snit. Tom, the engineer in charge at the Anchorage office, told me not to use the airplane. My boss in Denver overrode Tom's authority and told me to fly every morning to Deadhorse. I flew.

At one point there was talk about bringing in another airplane just for my personal use. Construction of the well was costing more than $8 million, but the thought of adding $50,000 a month just so the geologist could have his personal transport was a little too much for the parent company, Standard of Indiana.

In addition to my daily flight, we also flew search and rescue. You see, if any plane on the North Slope was off flight plan or disappeared, we were required to take off and look for it. My pilot and copilot, both members of the Alaska Air National Guard, appointed me official spotter.

I also had to periodically visit another wildcat well being drilled by Phillips Petroleum. Amoco owned a small interest, so I was instructed to fly over there once in a while, at my discretion, and check out the geology.

The first time I visited the Phillips well I got a big surprise. The airstrip being used by the rig was also the airstrip built for the Alaska Pipeline at Happy Valley. When we landed at Happy Valley I noticed a Learjet parked on the dirt strip. Upon inquiring, I found out that it was a charter service delivering personnel to the pipeline construction site.

"Can anyone book a seat on the Learjet?" I asked.

"Sure, just call our office."

Oh boy! When my tour was over, I was going to get my first ever ride on a Learjet.

The next day, when I called Denver from the RCA satellite phone, I had my secretary book the seat on the Lear for my departure date.

A week later, we "logged" the hole before setting three thousand feet of surface casing. Normally, the company wouldn't even bother gathering data, in the form of creating expensive wireline "logs" on a surface hole. But when you're already spending $8 million, what's an extra expense for a record of your work?

I was instructed to grab the paper copies as they were produced, climb in the Merlin, fly them to Anchorage, and personally make sure they were successfully faxed to Denver. I did what I was told.

We landed at Merrill Field and I drove a company vehicle to the office, my pilots in tow. Tom, the chief engineer and the project manager, rushed out of his office in a fury and, in front of the entire staff, Tom yelled at me: "Get your ass back to location immediately. And, give me those damned logs, I'll fax them to Denver."

"Sorry Tom, I have my instructions from Denver. I'm going to fax these here logs myself and," I paused for effect as I looked around the room, "when I'm done, I'm going to drive over to the Petroleum Club with these pilots and I'm going to drink a scotch and smoke a cigar."

After another pause, as Tom's bald head turned bright red, I added, "Maybe TWO scotches!"

When I was done with the fax machine, I walked out of the office, trying not to look cool. I may have even strutted a little like Napoleon.

About ten days later, I was getting ready to pack in and fly back to the "lower 48" (actually, I was heading to Honolulu to meet up with friends, but that's another story). The company man who ran the camp operation, and who in a wild coincidence had worked with my Uncle Dick on the Anchorage Police Force, stopped by my little lab/office.

"Ed, Tom has canceled your ticket on the Learjet. I know you can get it back, but for the sake of my friendship with your Uncle Dick, and the future of my job, could you please, for once, give in and not make a big stink? Please agree to fly back to Anchorage with the crew that is changing out the same day."

I agreed.

The next day was my last on location. That morning, I said good-bye to all my friends, drank coffee with the radio operator/weatherman in the weather station as I had done for six weeks, checked my bag for the last time, and walked down to the equipment pad. I wanted to be alone for a while before the company plane arrived.

That's where I was sitting, on a pile of drillpipe talking to two very large ravens about the wonderful adventure I had just had, when my pilots came walking by.

"Hi guys, Search and Rescue? Anyone in trouble?"

Jim looked at me thoughtfully. "A Texaco jet ranger is missing on Anaktuvuk Pass. The pilot and six geologists on board."

Whatever witty remark I might have made died in my throat. They walked over to the Merlin and took off.

I sat there for another fifteen minutes before I heard the engines of another and different airplane on approach to our dirt strip. The company plane landed. On a typical day, the crew would walk into camp and drink coffee and eat blueberry pie. That day, they climbed down from the cockpit, walked to the nose of the plane, and conferred among themselves. I could see their faces from where I was sitting.

I got up and walked over. "Hi guys, any word about the Texaco jet ranger?" I asked. They turned and looked at me.

"It was located ten minutes ago. All seven on board dead." The pilot paused, looked back at his crew of two, and back at me. "We weren't discussing the jet ranger. As we were on approach, we got word over the radio that the Learjet crashed on takeoff from Happy Valley. All on board are dead."

In a stunned and choked voice, I asked, "How many?" They said there was only one empty seat.

That was the first, but maybe not the last time that I was supposed to be on a flight that crashed.

—

Immediately after arriving back in Denver, Jackie and I drove up to Aspen, Colorado, and attended a meeting of the Eris Society in Snowmass. I was to give a talk on cooperative conservation. Eris is the Greek goddess of chaos. The Eris Society is a confused bunch of Libertarian thinkers and crackpots—a perfectly wonderful combination of brilliant logic and idiocy.

The second day of the meeting, July 30, found me at my computer early in the morning before the first session. I checked my email and got an awful shock from Raoul du Toit:

"Dear Friends, the helicopter, flown by John McTaggart, with Greg and Chris Foggins on board, crashed yesterday morning. Chris was in the open and fell beneath the helicopter as it went down. He is badly injured, but has been rushed to hospital and we are hoping for a complete recovery. Neither John or Greg in the front seats was injured."

The Robinson 44 following the crash that badly injured Chris Foggins.

I went pale and clammy. All I could think of was the oath. I had dodged another bullet. Less than two weeks after I flew in that damned chopper it went down. I didn't feel so hot. I walked to the end of the hall, out onto the grass at the verge of a ski run, and sat down to meditate.

The next morning, I felt a little better. As I sat down in front of my computer, my cell phone rang. It was Brent Haglund, president of the Sand County Foundation. I was hoping for good news from Africa.

"Ed, Mike Jones has crashed in a Cessna on takeoff from West Lunga. He is badly injured and is being attended on the airstrip by nuns from a nearby mission. There is no medevac service available and we need to get him out of there. Is there anyone you can think of with whom we can network in Africa?"

"I'll call my Zim friends in Boulder, but what about Urs Kreuter at Texas A&M? He's originally from Zim. Maybe he has contacts."

Brent agreed to call Urs. As luck would have it, Urs's brother in Johannesburg flies medevac for a South African firm. Mike was evacuated the next day to Lusaka. Lusaka looked him over and told the medevac they couldn't help. He was flown on to Harare. Harare medical, decimated by the Mugabe government, couldn't help. Mike was flown on to Johannesburg. He nearly died on the operating table. As the doctors were working on his shattered leg and arm his blood oxygen levels plummeted. His lungs had been flayed in the impact and he was bleeding internally. The South African doctors saved his life.

Darrell, the fellow I had met the previous year, died. He was in the backseat of the Cessna. His belly had been ruptured and he died of peritonitis. The pilot, Charles, his son, was not badly injured. How's that for a shitty experience for all involved. The fourth seat, left rear, was empty. That was to have been my seat.

I went back out to the ski run. I sat in meditation—a technique I had learned from my Buddhist monk son. I continued to meditate for days afterward.

I was alive. Nothing had happened to me. I had broken an oath, but I wasn't in the helicopter. What the hell was going on?

These were nonexperiences for me. But my friends were involved and I felt terribly touched by these events—as if I had been personally involved, if not responsible. I had tempted fate.

Remains of the Cessna airplane crash that nearly killed Mike Jones. Had I not missed the flight, I would have been in the backseat, which was completely destroyed in the crash.

It took me about ten days to emerge from my funk and resolve my feelings about the crashes. I decided I was okay with tempting fate.

So what if I die in a helicopter crash? If I spend the rest of my life in front of a TV watching other people have adventures and manage to die in my sleep, I'll still be dead, won't I? There's no telling which fate will take me. What's so bad about being killed by a stingray like Steve What's-his-face? At least you'll be remembered! I will bicycle with Cape buffalo and elephants. I'll work with the rhino team and fly in helicopters. I'll scuba dive with very large sharks. Hell, I'll even continue to do the really dangerous stuff like drive in Denver traffic.

So be it.

To hell with oaths.

CHAPTER 19

Camping Out on Tasha's Front Lawn

THE RHINO OPS GROUP IN Zimbabwe works mostly with animals on private conservancies. That's because almost all the rhinos on public lands have been poached. The private conservancies employ scouts to vigilantly protect the rhinos. So much for "government good" and the "private sector bad." In Zim, as of October 2013, there are more than five hundred rhinos on private conservancies and only about seven left on public lands.

When they can accommodate us, the conservancies let Rhino Ops use a safari camp. The lodgings can range in luxury from four stars down to a fly camp. One year, we camped out on Natasha's front yard.

Tasha lives on the Bubye River Conservancy, down the hill from Towla headquarters, Charles Davy's place. From the air you can see why Charles built here. The hill he is on is a very large and ancient granite kopje of low but massively impressive relief. The whole compound must cover twenty-five acres, but the granite is only exposed in a long slope in front of Charles's house. Elsewhere, huge quantities of soil had been hauled in for tree and shrub plantings, as well as large areas of grass where a helicopter can easily land.

I flew down from Harare with Raoul in the Husky, landing on the Towla airstrip where a white Lowveld Rhino Trust Land Cruiser pickup waited for us. John and I had helped Clive Stockil establish and fund the trust with money from the International Rhino Foundation (IRF), WWF, International Union for Conservation of Nature (IUCN), and individual donors.

We drove to Tasha's house. There, around the corner from the parking area, was a veritable tent city and RV camp, including John's camper trailer, a tiny tent for Chris Foggins, and various tents for participants like Chap Masterson, the young veterinarian who would eventually replace Chris Foggins; Lovemore Mungwashu of WWF who had become our regular spotter; and Lauren Leathem, a student veterinarian and the conservancy manager's daughter. I got Tasha's second bedroom—not sure how I got so lucky!

I threw my backpack on the bed and promptly took a walk around the property. The first sight was a collection of about twenty rhino skulls. It was like a mausoleum. Most skulls were missing their horns, which had likely been hacked off by poachers.

Rhino skulls are huge. They're even bigger with all the soft tissue attached. Rhino heads and shoulders, with their enormous muscles, appear to be about one-third the length of the whole body. The muscle attachments are fantastical. Rhino teeth are also pretty interesting. White rhinos—grazers—have massive, flat molars set in jaws that work in a side-by-side motion not unlike a cow. The molars of black rhinos—browsers—resemble carnassial teeth and they slide past each other in a shearing motion. The noise from a black rhino chewing is so distinctive and loud that, if you hear that noise in thorn-bush country, you should immediately climb a tree. At that range you might have a few seconds to react, but not much more.

Rhino skulls in front of Natasha's house; some natural deaths, many poached.

Each morning, we'd get up around 5:30 a.m., eat some porridge, and assemble our gear for the day. Tasha's staff would cook breakfast, make up pack lunches, prepare our dinner for serving between 5 and 10 p.m., and wash our filthy clothes. As soon as I figured out this simple routine, I began to pack differently.

I brought two pair of coveralls and two bush shirts. In fact, I brought two of everything, no more. For my feet, I'd bring one pair of Tevas (I wear the original "River Guides") and a pair of lightweight Merrell hiking boots. I'd rather walk in the Tevas, but after stubbing my toe on an acacia thorn, I was converted to closed-toe shoes. Top it off with a floppy hat, malarial drugs, binoculars, and a camera, and I was ready for Africa. Total gear weight: 22 pounds.

Operating out of Tasha's house on the Bubye River Conservancy, our first task was to find two young female black rhinos that had been hand-raised, their mothers having been poached for their horns. The young cows had been released about four months earlier but had headed right for the conservancy's eastern boundary, uncomfortably within reach of poachers and an easy getaway on the bordering tar road.

The lorry transport arrived the morning after I did and we set out. It didn't take long to locate the cows. They hung out together and were still pretty accustomed to humans. We decided to dart them, one after the other.

We divided the group into two teams and positioned ourselves nearby. Tasha (Charlie One) and I (Echo Mobile) were in one vehicle. Norman English (November Echo), the conservator of Save Valley Conservancy, and Graham (Alpha Two) was in the other vehicle with Blondie Leatham, the Bubye River Conservancy manager, and his wife, Katrina.

Those little girls (hey, they were not more than 800 pounds each!) stayed so close together that we darted them within a minute of each other. They also ran together and pitched over asleep within fifty meters of each other. We had to prepare them to be pushed and shoved (in the nicest way possible) into the transport container.

I was on "Lisa" within seconds, dragging a water canister to keep her cool. The veterinarian got the syringe of reversal drug in her ear, placed a rope around her hind leg and another around her neck, and the rest of the crew pushed to get her upright with her legs folded underneath her. Unlike white rhinos, blacks usually react to the reversal drug with something approaching alacrity, so we had to move fast.

Chris cried, "everybody ready?" He hit the plunger in the syringe, giving her a little squirt of the reversal drug, and up she popped like a wind-up toy. The guys pulled, we pushed, and she practically bolted into the container. That was easy!

As soon as the doors were closed, I hoisted the water canister onto my back and ran the short distance to "Carla." Within a few minutes, Norman had her ready to move and he administered a squirt of the reversal drug. Nothing happened. Her respiration fell to fifteen—that is, four breaths per minute—rather low.

Chris came over about then and took charge. Deciding we were already ready, he gave her the rest of the drug. Nothing happened. Respiration twenty. Uh, oh!

Chris whipped open his bag and grabbed a bottle of diprenorphine, filled a syringe, and gave her the whole dose. She let out a huge, extended sigh and her respiration rate picked up. We waited. It took more than six minutes to revive her. Chris figured that was the closest we'd come to losing a rhino in a decade. She finally staggered to her feet, her head wobbling drunkenly from side to side, and she walked docilely into the transport container. I hope her hangover wasn't as bad as I suspected it to be.

The translocation point was forty miles to the southwest. That's how big Bubye is. The drive took about five hours. Usually, translocated rhinos are placed in a boma for up to two weeks to make sure they forget their old home. This time, we just dropped them off and let them go. At last report, four years after relocation, they were still down in the south.

We spent the next day searching for baby black rhinos to catalog. When baby blacks are between twelve and twenty-four months old, the rhino team captures them and adds them to the list of known characters.

The capture is a little different from a translocation operation. The baby must be darted and the mother driven off by a helicopter or fixed-wing. We used to dart both mother and calf, but the vets decided it was too risky to dart the mother. She could remain slightly drugged and confused for many hours after revival, which put her and her calf at risk. Black rhinos are very conscientious mothers and always find their way back to their babies, usually within minutes if not a few hours. When separated, calves call to their mothers with pathetic bleating noises, helping the mother locate them. So rather than risk the lives of the cow and calf, Rhino Ops decided to risk the lives of its team. That's how committed we are to our work.

When the baby goes down and momma has been pushed at least a kilometer away, the team moves in. Besides the usual thermometer up the bum, blood-oxygen monitor on one ear, and reversal drug syringe in the other ear, several other activities (more or less upsetting to us amateurs) are executed. With an instrument that looks like an oversized pair of garden shears, the vet chops out "V" shape notches in positions along the beautiful fringed ears, effectively numbering the calf. If the rhino is number 387, it's notched in the 300, 80, and 7 positions on the ears. This allows aircrews to read the notches while flying fifty to one hundred miles an hour at a height of fifty to two hundred feet off the deck, even with the rhino twisting this way and that, passing under trees or through thorn bushes. It's amazing how accurate their readings are as a result of this system.

When the calf is numbered, the number is conveyed to Tasha, who records it. She also assigns each rhino a name, according to an alphabetical system. So, if momma is called "Blossom," her baby's name will begin with a B. It might be "Buttercup," "Begonia," "Bloom," or some such nonsense. In addition to ear notching, the team measures the baby, draws vials of blood for DNA testing and disease detection, and notches one toenail as an additional ID. Rhinos have been known to have their ears chewed off by hyenas, so backup precautions must be considered. Finally, a couple of those little microchips that ID your dog or cat are injected under the skin at the top of its neck.

I know the ear notching system really works, but I hate it. I feel so sorry for the baby rhinos losing big chunks of their beautiful ears. And the ears bleed a lot. The veterinarian treats the edges with potassium permanganate, which is an antiseptic and coagulant. Sometimes, I think my heart bleeds more than their ears.

My favorite job, aside from jet-washing rhinos, is painting them. Trust me, I have no artistic talent whatsoever, but for this gig I don't need it. Yellow paint is easy to see from the air, but wears off after a couple of weeks, allowing us to spot a calf we've already darted. So, among other things, we run around the bush carrying a pot of yellow paint. When the time comes, you unscrew the lid on the paint pot, fill the lid with paint, tear a small branch off a mopane or a shrub that doesn't have thorns, and paint the number on the rhino's back. Spots or swipes of yellow paint on your coveralls are a badge of honor.

Jackie painting a flower instead of a number on the backside of a black rhino.

In 2006, Jackie accompanied us for several days and took up the job of painting the rhino's back. During our mission, a call came from Sierra Oscar circling overhead. "Raoul, Raoul, John."

"John, Raoul!"

"Tell Jackie to paint the rhino's number on its back! I don't want to see any more flowers!" Her artistic interpretation was not appreciated.

Most years we try to put a few transmitters on adult rhinos. Way back when, Rhino Ops tried collars, similar to the ones successfully used on wild dogs, lions, elephants, and plains game. Several rhinos strangled on their collar and the others managed to scrape it off. If you look at a picture of a rhino, you will easily see why collars don't work. The rhino's enormous head is shaped like an inverted V—big across the shoulders narrowing to the point of its prehensile lip. They just don't work.

So, as an alternative, Raoul developed a technique for placing RFID transmitters into the rhino's big front horn. By the time I started working with them, the transmitter was about half the size of a point-and-shoot camera. Chris or John would auger out a hole in the side of the horn, cut the tip of the horn off, and then drill straight down the horn so the antenna would go up the hole and barely stick out the end. Epoxy, mixed on-site, would then be poured in the hole and covered with an ice pack. Epoxy is exothermic—it puts out a lot of heat—so ice is the only way to cool it. Once the epoxy has hardened, everything is cleaned up. We recover all the rhino horn shavings, and off we go.

The newest RFIDs are about the size of a camera memory chip container. The biggest problem with them is the battery capacity and transmission range, but technology is constantly improving. Someday we hope the chip will be really tiny—virtually undetectable by poachers. Wouldn't it be wonderful to have RFID receivers at airport security and catch the smugglers before they get out of Africa with their poached horn?

CHAPTER 20

Running with Rhinos

IN 2007, AFTER MONTHS OF planning, Jackie and I arrived in Harare. We stayed with Lin, Clive, and Lin's father Arthur at their home in Borrowdale Brooke. The Barrie house is a lovely brick structure with a tin roof surrounded by exquisite flower and vegetable gardens, all tended by Arthur, a retired Rhodesian Geological Survey topographer. Robert Mugabe lives around the corner, on top of the hill, so there's a little extra security in this neighborhood.

After a couple of days in Borrowdale Brooke, we drove into the Lowveld. We gave ourselves about a week to conduct business with Clive and the Save Valley Conservancy before Rhino Ops found their way to our doorstep at Senuko Ranch.

Just before Raoul, Tasha, and the rest of the crew arrived, we welcomed Dale Smith, a Canadian professor of veterinary medicine from Guelph University. She had brought her husband and children, a nine-year-old boy, and a thirteen-year-old daughter, making the safari into a vacation for the Smith family. Beka, the Smith's daughter, took a shine to me and me to her. She even went out in the field with us, following me wherever I went.

We threw ourselves into our work with the usual ballet of scouts, planes, trains, and automobiles. No, wait, it was more like planes, helicopters, and Land Cruisers.

There was very recent evidence that poachers had been tracking the old (forty-one years old according to records) white rhino bull that liked to live with a herd of Cape buffalo. Yep, he lived with buffalo. This old guy had been transported to Save Valley with the initial group from National Parks in 1993. He immediately busted through the fence on the western side of the conservancy and took up residence with the community's mombies. Until the fence was breached by invasions in 2005, in which Mugabe's people tried to reclaim the conservancy's land, he had remained there. Now he was back in the conservancy, but without friends among the few white rhinos in the area. So, he moved in with a large herd of Cape buffalo.

Two years before, in 2006, Jackie and I were getting ready for dinner at Senuko when we heard a terrific racket. A herd of buffalo was pouring into the water hole just in front of the lodge—there must have been five hundred of them. We grabbed our binocs and shimmied down from our chalet to watch from a slab of granite about forty meters from the water hole. The buffalo filled the water hole and started drinking. The sound was huge. *Slurp, slurp, bawl, bawl.* After a couple of minutes, we noticed a commotion on the west side of the water hole as an enormous white rhino waded through. The buffalo were pushing and shoving to get out of his way. He reached the middle of the water hole and flopped over on his side. We heard a loud sigh, "Ahhhhh." Then, he stood up and rolled over on his other side. He picked himself up again, drank for about five minutes, and walked off imperially. We noticed a light stripe running from his horn to his butt along the top of his back where he hadn't been able to get wet.

As the herd walked off a few minutes later, I saw more buffalo walking back to the water hole. I thought they were confused. Oh no, it was another herd, about three hundred more animals coming down to drink.

By the time they were done, they had lowered the level of the water hole by about half a foot!

So, due to the threat of poaching, Rhino Ops decided to dehorn the old fellow. I felt quite bad about this. I'm not convinced that dehorning deters poachers. Rhino horn grows about four inches a year. Horn is so valuable to poachers that they are known to kill rhinos after they'd been dehorned for what was left. Dehorning is still controversial, at least in my mind. Armed patrols are even more controversial, but I have no doubt that they work. In the eighteen months after the arming of scouts on two conservancies, twelve poachers were shot and killed, two more were wounded, and two were captured and sent to jail.

Down the road, I would raise the funds from conservation philan-thropists to arm the scouts on the Save Valley Conservancy. I tried to supply the guns from the United States, but the State Department refused export permits because they labeled Zim a terrorist govern-ment. The AR-15s were finally purchased in South Africa, at almost double the original price.

We found the lumbering white beast with no difficulty. We moved in quickly after he was darted. I'm sure Chris gave him a whopping-big dose of M99 but it acted on him more slowly than we expected. When we found him in a clearing, he kicked up a cloud of dust and charged us—in slow motion! *Thump, thump, thump. Snort.* Another cloud of dust.

He chased us, but we were much quicker than him and he was slow-ing down dramatically. Chris Foggins, carrying the white towel he used to cover the eyes of a rhino in order to keep them calm, walked right up to that monster and threw the towel over his eyes. Then he grabbed the nearly four-foot long front horn. And led him around by his horn!

The rhino refused to lie down. He stood there like a statue carved out of gray serpentine, the stone used by the locals for carving—like my Chipungu sculptures. Finally he settled back onto his haunches. Then we pushed until he knelt down. From there we carried out the routine, in addition to saw-ing off his horn about an inch from the base with a chainsaw.

Chris Foggins leading him into the open. He's asleep on his feet.
Astrid Heublin at far right, vet and former British Olympian.

In the process of being dehorned.

Rhino horn ready to transport by National Parks.

That horn is worth one-quarter of a million dollars in the Asian market. Once removed, the horns are turned over to a representative of National Parks who places them in a vault for storage. While in storage, they are subject to CITES inspections. CITES would shut down the whole Zim hunting industry if the horns were sold. So far the rhino horn is safe.

During the next week of operations, I watched the Canadian vet emerge from shy diffidence to leadership. After the first couple of days she was everywhere bossing all of us around. At least those who would obey her. Certainly, I did.

Around the tenth day of operations a call came in from the Chiredzi Conservancy about an hour northwest of Save Valley. They had located several rhinos they wanted us to check out, especially a baby that had been seen with several snares around its neck and legs. It didn't sound good.

The good news was that we were offered the use of Paul Tudor Jones's

Eurocopter, known as "The Leopard." The damn thing is appropriately painted in leopard spots. The helicopter can carry a big load, but it is too big for those little LZs the Robinson 44 can land on. Glendon, The Leopard's very experienced pilot, let Jackie and me ride with him and Chris on a darting run. I'm afraid the presence of a woman on board must have upset Chris. His first attempt at darting the rhino missed! I can only remember that happening once before.

The Leopard, Eurocopter on loan to Rhino Ops from Paul Tudor Jones.

Paul, an early developer of "hedge funds" and an American billionaire philanthropist, bought one of the premier cattle ranches and converted it into a conservancy—Malilangwe. With more than 130,000 acres, including leased lands, it borders Gonarezhou National Park. Paul turned "ownership" of the conservancy over to a locally held community trust. It was a clever move. Now, if the Mugabe government tries to dispossess him and steal his land because he is a white foreigner, he correctly argues that he owns nothing and that Malilangwe is "indigenous." Paul's conservancy was our test case for arming rhino patrols against poachers. It was from that initial success that nearly two million acres of private conservancies are now under the watchful eye of armed guards.

So, we were waiting on the banks of the Chiredzi River when the team finally located the injured baby and her mom. The sun was near setting, but Raoul was insistent that we move in immediately. He was afraid we would lose her overnight, so he ignored his own protocols about not starting an operation just before sunset.

What followed was a little unusual even for our Rhino Ops. We can normally get in close with the vehicles. The Lowveld is reasonably flat, so at most we have to maneuver around small drainages and patches of thick cover. It was not to be this time. We were still a long way off when we found ourselves blocked by thorn bush.

When I jumped out of the rear of that truck several things happened in rapid succession. Blake, one of the Chiredzi River owners, and our driver, ran off with the radio. I tried to follow but was hampered by the two kids trying to keep up with me. After a hundred meters, Chris appeared out of nowhere (The Leopard had set him down nearby) and handed me not one, but two heavy veterinary packs. I slung each over a shoulder and kept on running.

As I followed the sound of the helicopters, I tripped and face-planted. I picked myself up and promptly stepped through an acacia branch. There I was, running with 50 pounds of packs (I weigh 140), trying to keep track of two kids while taking a bead on helicopter noises from two helicopters. All the while, I was dripping blood. After what seemed like an eternity, I finally got my bearing from John and the Robinson 44.

I arrived at the site of the baby rhino just in time to see Blake being chased around a tree by the calf. Apparently he reached the calf a little early and the calf had been chasing him for about five minutes. Served him right for running out on me. Blake was ready to drop just as the baby conked out.

We did all we could in the field, but the situation was awful. The calf had a snare around his neck that had cut through his windpipe. The leg snares were equally bad. Ops made the difficult decision to remove the calf from its mother and doctor it. Fortunately, a Chiredzi River vehicle had come in from the opposite side and, driving over thorn bushes and small trees, had worked its way into the site. Natasha and Dale climbed in the back. Six of us lifted the calf and laid it in the bed of the truck. As the truck drove off, everyone began packing up. The sun had already set.

John McTaggart walked over. "Hey Ed, you don't want to spend five hours driving back to Senuko, do you?"

Why do I have a bad feeling about this? I thought.

"How about you fly back with me?"

We walked over to the helicopter. "I suspect you want more than my company, John. What is it?"

"Well, Ed, you know we're not supposed to fly after dark. I only have a small light on Lima Zulu [the Robinson 44] and the LZ back at Senuko Lodge is kinda tight. We have to land partly under a tree and next to an AVgas barrel. Hoping you can guide me in."

How I wished I'd never told him that story about how I hung halfway out of a helicopter window in Alaska, directing the pilot who was flying between the cloud tops and the trees.

We flew along in the gathering gloom. I noticed that John was flying a GPS bearing. That was comforting—as long as the GPS worked.

"So John, what's your alternative LZ if we can't tuck in by the car park?"

"You know that big grassy area a quarter of a mile toward the airstrip? I think that's big enough even if I can't see much of the ground."

"Uh, you mean the one on which that pride of lions has been living?"

"That's the one. I reckon they'll be out hunting, so no problem. By the way, Ed, I GPS'd your Land Cruiser when I flew back to find you. You ran five kilometers through some nasty thorn bush to get to the LZ."

"Well, I was a distance runner when I was young."

"You're over sixty, aren't you?"

"Yeah, I turn sixty-three next month."

We flew on. It's hard to be sure of your geography in the pitch dark, but I know the area well. I could just make out some lights in the vicinity of the workshops when Raoul popped onto the wireless.

"John, John. Raoul."

"Raoul, John."

"John, can you fly over the airstrip and check for animals. I can't see well enough even if I do a flyover."

I was shocked to hear the reply: "Sorry, Raoul. Can't manage it. See you back at the lodge."

We flew on. Nothing on the radio from Raoul. Five minutes passed. We were certainly parallel to the airstrip by now.

John got on the horn. "Raoul, Raoul, John."

Nothing.

"Raoul, Raoul, John."

We couldn't raise Raoul. My only positive feeling at that moment was that we hadn't seen an explosion in the direction of the airstrip. Nonetheless, my heart was in my boots.

Minutes later we were over the car park at Senuko. John slowed the helicopter and we slipped down between two granite kopjes and tucked the helicopter under a towering Acacia terminalis tree. I opened the window and leaned out, calling the distance to the green AVgas barrel.

"Four meters, three meters, three meters, two meters. Jesus, John, put her down!"

We landed just under two meters from the barrel.

"Piece of cake, mate," he said glibly.

Goddamned crazy helicopter pilot, I thought to myself, while at the same time admiring his skill.

"Let's go get cleaned up; I need a drink," I said.

"How about we find out Raoul's status first?"

We walked up to the office as Clive was coming out.

"Any word from Raoul?" John asked.

Clive smiled. "Dave was at the office so when he heard the plane he drove to the airstrip. He ran off a herd of wildebeest grazing about halfway down. Then he parked at the end of the strip with his headlamps on. Raoul got down with no trouble at all."

Another day, another dollar, I thought. *Wait one minute. I'm not getting paid to do this!*

CHAPTER 21

Romeo Hotel

IN 2009, I WAS CONTACTED by an American photographer. I had met her somewhere in my travels—Indonesia, I think—and had told her about Rhino Ops. Remember, I'm a storyteller. Me and my big mouth! She begged to be allowed to come along. I volleyed her to Raoul who allowed her to tag along with us to do a photo shoot.

When I arrived in Johannesburg, I passed through immigration and customs and out to the main terminal. John McTaggart and the redheaded photographer, Antonia, waited for me at the airport pub. They were drinking Tusker beer, if I recall correctly, and acted like they were old friends.

Antonia Stout isn't stout by my reckoning. She is a buxom, blue-green eyed redhead. She has that wonderful pink Irish complexion with just a trace of freckles that gives her a younger appearance than her thirty-something age. When she smiles, which is often, there isn't a man alive that wouldn't grin back at her like an idiot.

Hmm, I thought, *if she's having this effect on John and me, she's gonna have an interesting effect on the rest of the Rhino Ops guys.*

We stayed near the airport that night because we planned to fly John's Robinson 44 to Buffalo Range, Zimbabwe, at the crack of dawn the next morning.

When we arrived at the heliport, John looked at all our gear and said, "The two of you are going to have to pare yourselves down to one small bag each."

I assessed what was laid out. There were several packages that looked like veterinary supplies.

"Uh, John, what kind of drugs do you have there?"

He rattled off a bunch of chemical names. When he came to M99, I choked.

"We're smuggling opiates into Zimbabwe?"

"No problem Ed, we have 'hidey-holes' for the contraband."

Oh my god, I don't want to spend the rest of my life in an African jail, I thought.

"Uh, sure John. Got space for a coupla bottles of Macallan 12 scotch?"

"Just leave back another pair of socks and we'll be okay," he said as he showed me the hidey-hole. I dropped in the scotch.

The Robinson 44 is a four-seater, but it can only lift off with about 600 pounds of weight. Most of our stuff went into John's Mercedes, to be stored by his friend Penny. If I wasn't sure before, this trip confirmed that you only need two pairs of overalls, two shirts, and a sarong to work Rhino Ops.

The flight from Jo'burg to Buffalo Range is five hours, with a stop in Polokwane to clear RSA customs. As we approached the airport, John took out his radio frequency sheet and reset the radio to the Polokwane tower frequency.

"Romeo Lima Zulu to Polokwane tower. Do you read?"

No answer.

Antonia Stout, also known as Romeo Hotel, packing R44 for a flight from Jo'burg to Buffalo Range, Zimbabwe, 2009.

"Repeat, Romeo Lima Zulu to Polokwane tower, request clearance to land."

No answer.

John tried a couple more times.

The next thing I know, he sets the helicopter down in a farmer's field and shuts down. Fires up his cell phone and calls them direct.

"Hi, Polokwane tower. I can't raise you on your published frequency. Oh, you published the wrong number? Okay. What's the right number?"

John punched it into the radio. He fired up the Robinson 44, pitched our nose toward Polokwane. We got clearance and, instead of flying down the runway as required by law, we landed in the parking lot of the customs building.

The customs lady walked out to greet us. She carefully inspected the contents of the Robinson 44, including my backpack with my scant supply of clothes. She cleared us for departure.

We popped up in the air and flew over to the fueling station. From there to Buffalo Range was only a couple of hours heading over the north end of Kruger National Park and then over the Limpopo (what was once the "great gray-green, greasy Limpopo River," as Kipling called it, is now really more of a sandy, dried-out Limpopo), and across Gonarezhou National Park to Buffalo Range.

To my great shock, an immigration agent was waiting for us when we arrived in Buffalo Range, which has no regular flights. Silly me, there were Clive and Lin. They had arranged to drive the customs lady to the airstrip. Naturally, she had no transport of her own. I got my visa, a passport stamp, and a legal entry into a country with no hiccup for a change.

Romeo Hotel

Within a day of showing up at Senuko Safari Lodge, the team had given Antonia "Romeo Hotel" as her shortwave radio name. Either it stood for "redhead," or something more suggestive. She seemed to ooze sexuality.

Even Chris Foggins, who is older than dirt and all business, would look fondly her way after a couple of whiskies.

Early on in this operation, we found another white rhino bull, nearly forty years old according to the vets. We needed to treat him for an infected wound on the hump behind his head. Of course we measured his horn, while he was out. It was more than 120 cm! That's right, almost four feet long! I felt so sorry for the big old boy.

Romeo Hotel got her picture taken astride the rhino. I was shocked! No one had ever offered me a ride. I wonder why she got so lucky? Romeo Hotel changed the whole tone of Rhino Ops.

After a week in Senuko, we moved thirty miles north to Chishakwe (Shi-shock-way) Ranch, a subdivision of the Devuli Ranch, and pitched up at the De La Rue Ranch House.

Chris Foggins, retired head of Zimbabwe Veterinary service, our venerable vet; scotch, a present from me.

It's a really famous place, headquarters of the Devuli Ranch. Everything was left as is when they sold the property, including a library. I confess, I found a novel by Somerset Maugham that I not only read but also took with me when we left. De La Rue's signature is on the title page.

Dr. Rosemary Groom, the resident wild dog expert, occupied the little guesthouse next to the ranch. She had taken over the research on wild dog populations in the southeast Lowveld. Rosemary ("Whiskey Delta" to Rhino Ops) was an eligible twenty-nine-year-old wild dog fanatic living about as far away from a social life as any young woman can possibly get.

This particular two-week operation was distinguished by the amount of alcohol consumed. I ought to know, I picked up the tab.

Most of the booze seemed to be consumed in the form of scotch by Romeo Hotel and Alpha Two. That is, Antonia and Graham Connear, conservator of the Save Valley Conservancy. Graham was absolutely besotted by Romeo Hotel and spent as much time in her company as possible. Trouble was, no matter how much Graham drank, Romeo Hotel could outdrink him.

I have to admit that I kinda got in the spirit (as it were) of the thing, even though I'm the cheapest drunk around. About the third morning of this binge drinking, Graham dragged his sorry ass out at 5:30 a.m. only to find me up, washed, and so chipper that he likely contemplated murdering me.

In a vain, but failed, attempt to hide his frustration, he said, "How the hell are you so happy after last night? I've got the worst hangover. I'm gonna die for sure. And, there you are, grinning like an idiot."

"I'm only grinning because of the spectacle you make. Gra'm, you look like shit. And, whether you want to hear this or not, you're not getting lucky with Red. If only because you'd have to enter the bedroom she shares with Tasha. You walk in there and Tasha will break your head."

"Sheeit, man, my head's already broken."

—

I flew spotter that day. There was no way Raoul was going to let Graham in the Husky and puke.

Off we flew, me and Raoul. The temperature that day climbed and climbed until it hit 115 degrees Fahrenheit. I couldn't open the rear window because the wind would generate so much noise that no one would be able to hear anything through our sound-activated microphones. It's a good thing I wore my light-colored coveralls and stashed two half-liter water bottles for the six-hour flight.

Fortunately, I'm a desert rat and I don't mind flying in circles hours on end. Most folks get a might woozy after a few hours like that. I didn't even get thirsty.

About early afternoon, Chris darted a black rhino calf. We watched the baby while John drove the mother off with the helicopter. The baby finally sedated in very rough country. Nobody from ground crew was going to make it into that location. John set Lima Zulu down and Raoul and I circled in Sierra Oscar. Chris and John hauled all the gear over to the baby, all of ten meters from the helicopter LZ. As they worked, we continued to circle at about four hundred feet.

All of a sudden Raoul took Sierra Oscar into a near vertical dive. It was like we were flying a World War II mission and he was flying a Douglas SBD Dauntless dive-bomber rather than a Husky. Trouble was we weren't diving from twenty thousand feet! I finally caught a glimpse of the reason for our nosedive: The mother was charging straight at the helicopter, which was blocking her path to her calf. She was undeterred by its size—she was going to retrieve her baby. My eyes were glued to the Plexiglas window. More accurately, one eye plastered to the window. I couldn't have moved if my life depended on it. Actually, my life depended on Raoul, and his ability to maneuver the plane. He gunned the throttle before we hit the ground and steered the plane around.

About halfway through the maneuver, he said, "Ed, you okay back there?"

"Sure, Raoul. No problem. But, hey, could you warn me next time?"

"Next time is about now, Ed."

I grabbed my shoulder harness and hung on. We dive-bombed the cow a second time. This time I could hear the engine growling and the high-pitched whistle of the air forcing its way through the seams of the windows. Fortunately the cow spun around, kicked into gear, and high-tailed it back the way she came. We followed her for about three kilometers, circling and diving time and again to keep her in front of us and moving away from the calf. I'm certain there were times we were below the treetops. After a few minutes, we turned back to the worksite.

Before wrapping up operations for the day, we continued to scout for rhinos for another two hours. Our airtime was six hours total.

When I climbed down that evening (well, really I wriggled out of

Several of the African painted dogs of Bedford Pack, Chishakwe Ranch,
Save Valley Conservancy, 2009.

the seat and slid to the ground), my coveralls were completely soaked through with sweat.

"That was fun!" I said to Tasha, waiting by the Land Cruiser. She looked me up and down and asked, "You want a beer or a shower first?"

"A beer, please. I have to rehydrate!"

The morning of the third day at Chishakwe, Rosemary stopped by the office early and invited me to visit the "Bedford Pack"—the wild dogs she was studying—with her. Raoul looked over the top of his computer. It was 6 a.m. and he was already working.

"Go ahead," he said, "you'll find it interesting."

CHAPTER 22

Whiskey Delta and Wild Dogs

I HAD SEEN WILD DOGS in Botswana and Zambia as well as Zimbabwe. Our friend Lin Barrie, the painter, often assisted wild dog researchers and had spent a lot of time with the "Senuko Pack," down in the south end of the conservancy.

A couple of years earlier, just before arriving at Senuko, Lin excitedly emailed us about the ten pups she'd discovered being raised by the Senuko Pack. When we drove down a couple of weeks later, she was heartbroken. "A python got into the den a couple of days ago and ate six of the ten pups."

It was an old ant bear (aardvark) hole. The alpha female, trying to defend her litter from the encroaching python, had picked up one pup at a time and carried it off to another abandoned ant bear hole close by. She was able to return three more times before the python finished off the sixth pup.

I had Lin stop at the den and halfway crawled into the hole. I studied the track of the python for a while and determined that it wasn't in there. Then I tracked it away from the den, hoping to locate it. I didn't want to hurt the python, mind you. Eating pups is a python's day job. I just wanted to check it out. The python had slithered up a small granite kopje, presumably returning to its own den. Since black mambas also den on granite kopjes, I abandoned the trail.

Americans see nature as benign. That is mainly because: (1) we live in cities and don't know dick about nature, and (2) we killed off most of the predators in North America, so we almost never see the "killing zone." But nature isn't like a Disney movie. Nature is brutal. "Red in tooth and claw" ain't half of it.

Even Bambi-like animals—impala, for an African example—display dominance in what humans anthropomorphize into nasty behavior. A doe impala is fully capable of pronging you with its horns or driving its front hooves right through your chest. And, never approach an antelope in rut. They are too dangerous! I'd rather stick with rhinos, thank you very much.

Furthermore, the animal responsible for more death, destruction of property, and transmission of disease in the United States is Bambi itself, the white-tailed deer. It kills more than three hundred people a year, causes millions, maybe even billions, of dollars in property damage from auto wrecks to lost crops, and carries Lyme and chronic wasting disease. Yet our current regulatory system of trophy hunting cannot properly manage deer populations.

White-tailed deer are also severely hindering the regrowth of US Midwest and eastern forests, which are in crisis due to the old growth reaching the end of its life cycle. The American people along with their government agencies have stuck their collective heads in the sand. We desperately need to reduce white-tailed deer populations but no one has the courage to look at the big picture. What we need is culling on the scale of Save Valley Conservancy.

Let's not call it "commercial hunting," because it's not that. It's culling, and a tremendously beneficial consequence would be the meat we would have. I would assert that between the white-tailed deer and Canada geese (another pest) populations of North America, we could feed all the homeless in the United States. In 2005, Save Valley Conservancy culled 7,000 impala out of a population of 25,000. Every animal was harvested for meat, which fed the staff, the local communities, and even me.

While we were there, we went out in search of the cause for the deaths of 80 percent of the Senuko Pack. It had run through a snare line set up by poachers to catch impala. Three dogs had died in the snares, where they were caught. The poachers don't eat dog, so they left them. We picked up as many snares as we could find and added them to the thousands piled high back at the workshops.

—

One evening, Clive and I were watching a family of chacma, or Cape baboons, in a tree as the Senuko Pack ran by on their way to their den site. The baboons didn't utter a sound.

"Clive, I thought baboons always scream a warning when predators come by?"

"Actually, Ed, baboons know that dogs don't hunt them. So, they don't care. Cats hunt and kill baboons on the ground, and leopards hunt them up in their nesting trees. If a cat comes by they kick up the fantastic racket that you've heard from the lodge." He imitated a baboon: "Yahoooo, yahoooo, yahoooo."

Wow! I had no idea baboons distinguish between thems-that-eat-them and thems-that-don't.

The Bedford Pack

It's almost impossible to follow wild dogs on a hunt. They run too fast to follow, sometimes splitting up, sometimes staying together. So, we hung around the den and watched for the adults to return.

The Bedford Pack is the largest painted dog pack ever recorded on Save Valley Conservancy. In 2009 it numbered forty-two dogs. The most amazing part was that the alpha female had given birth to eleven pups, which were about eight weeks old when I saw them. A beta female birthed six pups about four weeks later. Rather than killing the beta pups, as wildlife biologists had suggested was always the case, the alpha female nursed all seventeen!

African painted dogs have a special feeding behavior: they gulp down chunks of meat and hold the whole mess in their stomachs until they return to the den, when they regurgitate pieces to feed their pups. I had seen this behavior before, but among many adults and few pups. This time, when one adult got back to camp, she was overwhelmed by seventeen yipping, licking, tumbling, hungry pups. She barfed up chunk after chunk of meat until she was tapped out. The poor dog was exhausted. She slumped away and flopped down in the grass. In came the next adult and the circus was repeated. Not a single adult kept its whole meal. When the pack had finally finished feeding the pups, there wasn't an adult left standing. Even the alpha male, who usually stands guard, couldn't muster the energy to carry out his primary job. But the pups were up! Still yipping and harassing the poor adults, they were indulged to such a great degree that your heart swelled with love for these skinny, stinky (and boy do they stink), colorful canids.

Wild dogs have a terrible reputation. Farmers hate them. They kill game, including goats and other domestic stock whenever possible. Wild dogs weigh only about 30 pounds but can take down antelope much larger than themselves. Around Chishakwe they were felling kudu weighing up to 400 pounds. Their bad rap likely originates in their hunting of livestock, but also their hunting style, which is gruesome at best. They run down their prey as a pack from behind and hamstring and/or rip their guts out. Then they eat their prey alive.

I think they are magnificent. I've seen adult wild dogs feeding injured adult members of their pack as they would their pups. You won't see that happen with lions or hyenas. If you are a lion and you can't eat, you starve to death. Not with wild dogs. They really take care of each other.

Whiskey Delta drove me around in her field vehicle, a decrepit four-wheel-drive Ford pickup.

"Rose, your truck won't last another year. You need a Land Cruiser," I commented.

Within the year, she was driving a new Uri, a Land Cruiser clone built in South Africa. That's right, I bought her a vehicle. She worked her magic on me, too.

—

Just before dinner, I saw John leave Rosemary's place. Before I could start making wrong assumptions, I noticed that he was carrying two bottles of booze in each hand.

"Hey John, watcha doin' there?" I asked.

"We're runnin' low on scotch, so I raided Rose's larder," he responded, dispelling any untoward assumptions.

That evening, shortly after drinking commenced, I noticed that Rosemary was vying with Romeo Hotel for the attention of the boys. She was jealous! How wonderful! Go, go, girls. Duke it out!

Later that evening, when my hearing was affected by my high blood alcohol level, I could have sworn I heard Whiskey Delta address Antonia as "Foxtrot Romeo Hotel."

I sloshed over to John, who was still with us that evening (previous evenings he had been retiring before most of the fun happened) and whispered, "John, did Rosemary just call Antonia . . . ?"

He grinned back at me. "Eddie, she's certain that Red dyes her hair."

"Oh, 'Fake Redhead,'" I mumbled and dragged myself off to bed.

The next day we encountered a serious crisis. The scouts reported a rhino cow poached north of Chishakwe. They had picked up the track of poachers and followed them for several hours. The scouts heard gunshots and found the cow. She had been shot once through the head by an AK-47 and her horn had been chopped out with a panga. Worse yet, the cow had a nearly grown baby and a newborn. The older baby had charged the poachers, who had responded in kind by spraying the area with submachine-gun fire, hitting both youngsters.

Now you must understand that the scouts could make out this entire story by spore, blood, and shell casings left around the site. They tried to call in support on their radio. Its battery was dead.

They ran the entire way back to Sanga and called us at Chishakwe with the news. They reported over the phone that the poachers were four guys who had run off toward the nearest tar road.

Raoul was hopping mad.

"John, get the helicopter up. I'll get in the Husky. We need to find these guys before they make it to the tar road."

John just stared at Raoul.

"Uh, guys. This isn't Hollywood," I said. "One round from an AK-47 can bring either one of you down."

I wasn't finished.

"Call in the cops and send the trackers back out. Maybe we can figure out where they're headed and cut them off. But, please, not in the aircraft."

The poachers got clean away. When they ran north to the tar road, they ran inside each other's tracks, obscuring their telltale trail. That technique and their AK-47s were indicators that they were Zimbabwean Army for sure.

The next day, the scouts found the younger of the two babies. She was immobilized for evaluation in the field. Natasha and Chris found two entry wounds. One was a "through-and-through," just above her ankle. The other was bad news: a wound entering the upper back and angling downward into her gut. There was no exit wound and no way we could operate in the bush.

We loaded her onto a Land Cruiser and shipped her off to the Bubye River Conservancy five hours away. They would keep her under observation at the orphan rhino nursery. Natasha was dispatched to travel with her.

Later reports had the older baby recovering on her own, but the little calf succumbed to the gunshot and died within a week.

Field dressing a wounded black rhino baby shot by poachers on Chishakwe Ranch, SVC; it died, 2009.

—

As we wrapped up the two weeks of Rhino Ops, I checked in with Raoul.

"What does the booze bill come to?" I asked.

"I was just adding it up. Counting Coke and beer, it comes to $1,100."

"Jesus! There were only seven of us!"

I stuck my hand in my pocket and peeled off eleven Ben Franklins. In all my years working Rhino Ops, that's the only time we drank like that. Blame it on (Foxtrot) Romeo Hotel.

CHAPTER 23

Lions, Lions, Everywhere

IN JUNE OF EACH YEAR, I am usually busy preparing for my annual summer activity, running the Philmont Scout Ranch Volunteer Geologist Program. It is one of my many beloved odd jobs. I organize fifty professional geologists from the United States and abroad to teach earth science at the Boy Scouts of America's largest national high-adventure base.

—

Located in the Sangre de Cristo Mountains of northern New Mexico, Philmont puts about twenty-two thousand boys and girls through a twelve-day backpacking program every summer. Yep, BSA is co-ed. Philmont is 137,000 acres. Most donated by Waite Phillips, an Oklahoma oilman in the 1920s. Philmont now uses the ranch, another ranch it rents, parts of the Carson National Forest known as the Valle Vidal, and a few chunks of Ted Turner's Vermiejo Ranch for the backpacking program. All in all, the kids have access to almost 250,000 acres. Geologists give up their vacation time and pay their own way to Cimarron, New Mexico.

As I prepared for Philmont 2012, I got a panicked email from Raoul.

"The Husky needs a new exhaust assembly to pass inspection. The bitch running Aviat's shipping department won't send the part. Susie Ellis at IRF has guaranteed the payment, but nothing seems to move her. Rhino Ops isn't going to happen unless I get the goddamn part."

Whew.

I emailed back. "Hi Raoul. What can I do for you?"

Raoul replied, "Aviat is in Aston, Wyoming. You're a big deal in Wyoming. Do something."

I'm not a big deal in Wyoming. But I have friends who are. I called Indy Burke, director of the Ruckelshaus Institute at the University of Wyoming and, incidentally, a director of the Sand County Foundation like me.

"Indy, help. Call the university president, call the governor, call God, but help me get this part to Raoul in Harare," I demanded frantically.

"Hi, Ed. Calm down," she replied. "Why would I call the governor?"

Indy listened to the story of Raoul's exhaust pipe.

"Not a problem. I'll call her myself."

"Oh, okay."

"I'll get back to you with the details."

"Uh, roger that."

Indy, a rangeland ecologist, runs one of the largest, most successful programs in the country that trains young resource managers how to work collaboratively with all sectors of the conservation community. She is extremely well connected. She combines jogging with hunting elk. Indy and I are buds.

The next morning, the phone rang. It wasn't a recording begging me to vote for someone, it was Indy.

"All right. Taken care of."

"Tell me how you did it," I said.

"I told the nice lady who I am and how important Raoul's program is to the University of Wyoming. That's all it takes in Wyoming. Everyone loves the university. The part will be shipped today."

The part was shipped, but the company packed it in the biggest box they had. Shipping cost the rhino project $500. So, if the president of Aviat reads this story, please send your $500 contribution to: The International Rhino Foundation, c/o Raoul du Toit.

I contacted Raoul with the shipping information and got a return email.

"Ed, could you also bring along some spare gauges for the Husky? I'm having them shipped to your home."

I've become so good at smuggling that they take it for granted that I will risk going to prison for them.

—

As usual, upon my arrival in Harare, Raoul picked me up after my stroll through customs.

"We may be able to get off [the ground] tomorrow. I'm waiting on the paperwork approving the Husky inspection. It's been two weeks. The official in charge is going slow."

Let me translate: Raoul would not pay a bribe, so it could take however long it takes the official to get around to showing up at his office and countersigning the paperwork. Welcome to Zimbabwe.

Sure enough, Raoul was near to pulling out his sparse hair, having been waiting on the official for two weeks. He finally got the paper at 3 p.m. the day after I arrived. We loaded up his truck and drove to the airport. Used to be, you dragged your plane out of the hangar at Charles Prince Airport and took off. Now, you have to go through security, file a flight plan with the tower, fill out paperwork, and pay a fee for any passengers in order to be allowed off the ground. We took off about an hour before sunset.

As we flew south toward "the dam," Raoul radioed to me. "Ed, we have a thirty-knot headwind. Our ETA at Ripple Creek will be about forty minutes after sunset."

The Ripple Creek airstrip at the Bubye River Conservancy is unattended and unlit.

"Do you think we ought to try it?"

What the fuck? Is he really asking me that? I thought.

Instead of that, I replied, "Raoul, you're the pilot. It's entirely up to you."

"Let's turn back."

"Ask the tower to call Deleen and I'll take you both out to dinner."

Over dinner, Raoul told me about receiving the Goldman Environmental Prize in 2011 and meeting Barack Obama at the White House.

"There I was at this reception in the West Wing of the White House hosted by President Obama. He asked me if there was anything he could do for me. I told him that I was worried about future budget cuts in our funding from US Fish and Wildlife Service. He promised to help. Then, I asked him if I could do something for him—like solve the national debt."

Raoul paused, his nearly black eyes twinkling.

I already knew the answer, but I had to ask.

"Okay, Raoul, just what was it you told Barack?"

He grinned and said, "It's not what I told him, it's what I gave him. I pulled out of my jacket pocket a one-hundred-trillion-dollar Zimbabwean bill and gave it to him." Then I said, "There. Now, you can pay off the national debt."

—

The next morning we were out just before sunrise. On our approach we flew along the southern edge of Ripple Creek Dam. On the approach to the airstrip, I could see the Mitsubishi M-2 airplane that had crashed earlier that year.

"Raoul, isn't that Charles's [Charles Davy] M-2 half off the runway?"

"Yeah, Ed. The nose wheel collapsed on landing. For several years we've been telling Charles that the M-2 comes in way too fast for a dirt strip. Now, he knows it for sure!"

We set down, missing the Mitsubishi by the expediency of using the other half of the airstrip to land. I walked over to the M-2 to check it out. The impact had driven the port landing gear up into the passenger cabin.

Dear, dear. I hope no one was sitting in that seat, I thought, looking at the steel strut that was sticking up through the bottom of a seat like a spear.

After rolling out drums of aviation gas for a half hour and loading them onto the back of pickup trucks, we were ready to go. The Husky fuels up at the airstrip, but we resupply the Robinson 44 from drums carried by truck anywhere we can—usually two or three times a day—mostly at water holes, sometimes at any treeless wide spot on the savanna where it can land.

*Refilling RLZed in the bush from a petrol barrel; note "Rhino"
name painted on barrel, 2012.*

Bubye River Rhino Operations have settled down to cataloging babies, with a few transmitter insertions thrown in. That's because it's found the way to cut down on poaching. Arm the scouts; kill the poachers. In two years, twelve poachers have been killed and two wounded on the southeast Lowveld conservancies. The South African poachers have fled back to safer ground in their home country (more than eight hundred rhinos have been poached in RSA during 2013, only ten in Zim). The Zim poachers have ducked for cover as well.

I raised about $25,000 US in 2012 for the purchase of automatic weapons for Save Valley scouts. I ran all my traps with the US State Department to no effect. Zimbabwe, according to the party line, is a "terrorist nation" and so they would not grant an export permit. Then I reached out to the president of Fabrique Nationale d'Herstal in Belgium. No help. We finally bought the guns in RSA, all legal, at a higher price. Still, on that special page in my CV, I now list another odd job: "gunrunner."

I know, it's a bad joke. But it looks so good underneath "smuggler."

Recently, I had to send my CV to Indonesia for my role in a Nature Conservancy research project assessing resources of a new protected marine area around the Savu Sea, south of the island of Flores. When Rod Salm, marine biologist and senior scientist for TNC Indo/Pacific, saw my CV he just about choked. I begrudgingly deleted the "Odd Job" page and resent it. Rod was sure the Indonesian government would not appreciate my sense of humor. Smuggler and gunrunner, indeed!

The Ripple Creek Safari Lodge we used that year was a little rundown. Among its shortcomings was a lack of mosquito netting. The first night, John and I, sharing a room, got bitten up badly. The next day we had mozzie nets shipped in. I didn't get malaria, but the risk was unacceptable. Thus arose my new motto: Trampled by rhino? okay! Malaria? No way!

Working in the north end of Bubye River Conservancy had its own flavor. The first day we pitched up at a water hole waiting for instructions. As usual, I started walking around, looking for a nice flat, shady spot to lie down and take a nap. I learned quickly to catch up on my sleep any way I could while waiting on the scouts to find a rhino.

Natasha called me back to the truck. "Ed, you might want to stay close to the truck. The lions are really active around here and might just be watching."

I walked away and circled the water hole. On the other side, I found the skull of a giraffe. Then, more bones. Finally, I found a femur.

Wow, I thought, *the lions are hunting giraffes. That's very impressive!*

I picked up the big bone and walked back toward the truck. In the shade of a little mopane tree, I lay down and used the thighbone like the Japanese use a headrest. I was asleep in about thirty seconds.

We did run into lions, but only at dawn and dusk. Otherwise, the lions were hard at work at their day job: sleeping.

The 2012 Rhino Ops was something of a disappointment—the team was just too damn efficient! We had a total of eighteen rhino babies to process and we did fourteen in the first three days.

On day two we handled eight rhinos, an all-time record for the crew. I had booked my trip for twenty-one days. By day eight we had cataloged all the babies, located and tagged a few white rhinos that hadn't been cataloged previously, and attached a few transmitters.

"I'll call my secretary and have her rebook your return, Ed. But, first, let's make a plan for you to see some of the country with me." By that, John meant that we could go geologizing for a couple of days so he could, once again, get some free consulting out of me.

So, he invited me to Falcon College, the private boy's school he runs. John is an "old boy" at Falcon. His sons went there, and he volunteered to be the CEO when called upon. Naturally, we landed the helicopter on the football field.

Back in 2000, Guy Barber had flown me over Falcon College on the way to Barberton Lodge on the now destroyed Bubiana Conservancy. He buzzed the old gold mines nearby, noting that they were "worked out."

"Not with American technology," I immediately replied.

Now, twelve years later, John was negotiating with a foreign mining company to reprocess the dumps and open the old underground mine—using technology developed in the United States and Germany.

We spent a couple of days visiting the Falcon gold deposit and some chromium dumps on the Great Dike. The Great Dike is a band of iron- and magnesium-rich rocks formed about two billion years ago when mantle was trapped and squeezed during the collision of two continents. Africa is so deeply eroded that the Great Dike is exposed at the surface, extending from northern South Africa, beneath the Kalahari Sands in Botswana, across Zim, through the northwest corner of Mozambique, and into southern Tanzania. It is one of the world's biggest sources of platinum, chromium, nickel, and serpentine. There is a belt like this where the Indian subcontinent crashed into Asia, but it still sits about seventeen miles beneath the Tibetan Plateau. I'm afraid that the sub-Himalayan ore bodies won't be exposed until the sun is about to go nova, maybe three billion years from now.

After playing geologist for a couple of days, John dropped me off at the Safari Club in Bulawayo, a wonderful, if moldy, old club converted into a hotel. Full of nineteenth century memorabilia, it was nearly empty. Before John took his leave, we hit the bar and made ourselves a couple of shandies from beer and lemonade—very refreshing.

What? You expect a barkeep to be found in the bar? Well, we didn't wait for him.

That evening, I ate dinner in a fantastic colonial dining room. I was all alone. There wasn't another soul in sight. Naturally, I ordered something dangerous: piri piri (African bird's eye chili pepper) chicken livers. If it hadn't been fresh, it probably would have killed me. The food was terrific and, even better, I lived to tell about it.

The next day I hired a driver to take me to a safari lodge on the border of Hwange National Park. The drive cost me more money than a round-trip ticket from Bulawayo to Johannesburg! That's Zim for you: you can't expect to take the bus.

I stayed at Ivory Lodge for a couple of days and found it intolerably boring to go on game drives with tourists. Impala, elephants, and a lion, oh my! More like, "ho hum!"

The saving grace was their hide, or blind, as Americans would call it. I waited until everyone was asleep and crept down from my chalet hoping not to run into a pride of lions. From the hide I watched a breeding herd of elephants, sometimes so close that I could have whacked one with a biscuit.

John and Amanda joined me from Falcon College and we spent a day together. We sat around the campfire at night and told war stories to each other. They weren't interested in going on game drives either.

CHAPTER 24

The Definition of a
Great Adventure

WHILE I WAS WAITING TO hear from Raoul as to the exact timing of Rhino Ops in 2013, a company in North Carolina was trying to produce new receivers that would extend the range of the latest transmitters from about four hundred meters to more than five kilometers. The tech department wasn't satisfied with the tests, and they seemed to go on interminably.

When I finally received the new equipment via FedEx, the package contained nothing more than two screw-in antennas.

What the hell?

I emailed Raoul. He hassled the company. At the last possible moment they shipped me the two plastic receiver cases and forty little transmitters. The boxes were so large that I could barely squeeze one in my backpack and the other in my little rolling bag. I was traveling "carry-on only" and I was miffed. There was no room for my clothes. Finally, I opened the boxes.

There was nothing inside! The dumb shits had shipped the empty receiver cases without the guts. I filled the boxes with my clothes. If I got caught by customs, so what. What were they going to charge me with, smuggling empty plastic boxes? I felt pretty foolish.

Well, I said to myself, *I suppose this will count as "smuggling practice."*

As I went through customs at Harare, I made friends with a lovely young woman in the visa line. I waited for her as if we were traveling together and we wandered over to the baggage carousel. I didn't have any checked bags, but I wanted to watch the customs agents. As soon as I saw all three of them occupied with passengers, I said good-bye to the young lady and walked through the "Nothing to Declare" line.

I walked right out of the terminal and waited for the white truck with "Lowveld Rhino Trust" painted on the side. After about five minutes it pulled in about twenty meters from me. I walked over. Raoul's wife Deleen was driving.

"Hi Deleen, what's up?"

"Raoul is as sick as a dog. Looks like he's coming down with the flu."

Not the news I wanted to hear. I got sick the year before by kissing Tasha. Now I was going to be in the cockpit of a teeny, tiny airplane with another (and less attractive) infectious agent.

We drove to their house. I didn't see Raoul until the next morning.

"Hi, Sport," I cheeped cheerfully. "What's got you sicker, the flu or the empty boxes I carried nine thousand miles from the States?"

Deleen piped up. "You should have heard him on the phone, Ed. I went straight to the garden, so I couldn't hear him."

Raoul looked sheepish. "I was highly annoyed and gave them a real 'what for.'"

Less than two hours later we were in the Husky heading south to Bubye River Conservancy. This year we'd be working off of a short dirt airstrip. Natasha was waiting for us when we landed.

"What do we have this year, Tasha?"

"We've identified twenty-two black rhino calves between twelve and twenty-four months old."

"That's four more than last year," I said, congratulating her. We'd once again be cataloging youngsters.

Our 2013 camp was another hunting lodge, Samanyanga, in a

different area of Bubye River Conservancy. The helicopter El Zed was parked in the sandy bottom of the Bubye River right in front of the main house. As usual, the inside of the house was stuffed with food boxes, veterinary supplies, backpacks, and computers. Chap had a separate table to process blood samples. A large dining room table took up the rest of the great room.

We got ready for the first job. The radios started to squawk. Raoul and Lovemore drove to the airstrip. The rest of us started to pack the helicopter.

Tasha turned to me and said, "Ed, we're not using a vehicle and there is no room in the helicopter."

She must have registered my dismay and remembered her manners. "Sorry," she offered.

I was stunned. I'd just traveled twenty-one hours across the world to be with my team, and they summarily dismissed me with a belated "sorry."

So, for the next two days I traveled with Jackson Kamwe and his Charlie scouting team. The scouting teams were composed of between five and seven scouts, clad in uniforms of modified military kakis and black combat-style boots. Several scouts on each team were armed with 5.6 mm AR-15s—the type of guns I purchased for Rhino Ops! The bad guys are typically armed with 7.6 mm AK-47s, so if a shootout occurs the authorities can distinguish between the scouts and the poachers.

Jackson is possibly the most famous black scout in Africa. Certainly, the most famous black rhino scout. He used to work for Clive Stockil (and therefore, me, I suppose), and I've known him for years. He is a joy to be around.

On this trip he showed me how the trackers pick up the spore of rhinos. We drove off to a water hole where the scouts walked around the water hole and picked up the fresh spore of a black rhino cow and baby. Charlie 5 and Charlie 6 took off cross-country. They were gone for six hours before they finally closed in on the two rhinos. At each stopping point, I got out and walked out with the trackers. I only looked like I was studying rhino spore. In point of fact, I was looking for porcupine quills.

On the second day with the scouts, I was again wandering around looking for porcupine quills, when the guys called out to me. They had located a large and very skinny African rock python under a shrub. He was about three meters long—about half the size of one I wrestled with in Hwange National Park a dozen years ago. I peeked under the branches, reached in, and grabbed him around the middle and dragged his sorry ass out into the open. He raised his head and hissed at me, as snakes are wont to do. That gave me the opportunity to grab him behind the head.

Charlie scouting team: Natasha Anderson (left), Jackson Kamwe (right).

The scouts took turns taking pictures of the snake and me; there was no way they were going to approach it themselves. Every black African I've worked with, from the Maasai in Tanzania to the Shangaans in southeast Zimbabwe, has been terrified of snakes. Not that they don't have a right to be cautious, of course. The savanna is home to Egyptian cobras, vipers like the puff adder, and, worse by far, black mambas. And pythons have been reported to have swallowed small children and tried to swallow adults.

I'm not afraid of snakes, generally, and certainly not pythons. I'm not even scared of cobras, spitting or otherwise. But I have great "respect" for the black mamba, that is, I keep the hell away from them. They're very aggressive, can reach sixteen feet in length, and are poisonous to beat the band. A friend of mine lost two horses to mamba bite. As the horses fled its company, the mamba struck each as it passed. Think about it: that black mamba had enough venom in its poison glands to kill two full-sized horses. My, my, that's a snake to be feared.

I've handled venomous snakes on occasion. The nonvenomous variet-ies tend to be easier to catch by hand. The real trick is to identify them correctly, and they're even easier to handle when they're distressed. In this case, it was also early morning in winter, so the snake was a little sluggish from being cold.

This poor python hadn't eaten in months. In fact I've never seen such a skinny python. Still, you might say, those are no reasons to go wres-tling a python. On the other hand, my "bravery" earned me real cred with the scouts, who had a slightly different opinion of this mzungu after the snake encounter. They no longer treated me like just another dumb tourist! Maybe they now call me "Snake Eddie" behind my back.

Rock python I pulled out of the shrubbery for the "enjoyment" of Charlie scouts, 2013.

The next day, two young vets arrived at our lodge. Lauren had worked for us the year before as an intern. Now she and her new husband, Kobus, were on holiday. Tired of small animal practice, they joined us for five days of rhino fun. The three of us became the Rhino Ops ground crew, using their Land Cruiser for human and fuel transport.

On their last day with us, we were running low on rhino babies to catalog, so we decided to spend the day working on white rhinos. There are quite a few white rhinos on Bubye River Conservancy that have not been ear notched. Notching the babies presents something of a problem for the team, since white rhino cows are rather stupid compared to black rhinos. Once a white rhino starts running it may not stop for a long time, so when driven from their young they are fully capable of forgetting about them. The scouts once logged a bull that ran more than thirty miles before he pulled up to munch some grass.

A year-old white rhino calf will certainly die without its mother. Lions or hyenas will pick it off within a couple of weeks. Thus, the team waits until calves are almost two years old before cataloging—just in case the mom and calf are permanently separated. A twenty-four-month-old white rhino calf is hardly a baby, weighing in at around 2,500 pounds. We managed to ID four white rhino calves that day, ranging from twenty to twenty-eight months old.

As I mentioned earlier, white rhinos react to the drugs with a whole lot less aggression than blacks. With the huge white babies, the crew would just back off fifty meters and stand around as the vet reversed the M99. The calf would stand up, stagger this way and that way, snort a few times, shake its head, and start to meander around the thorn bushes. They're just not all that aggressive, even when not sedated.

Doing four white rhino calves in a row had an unintended consequence on the last calf of the day, an 800-pound female black rhino. After all these years of working together, the team just kinda forgot what it was doing.

The baby went down about four hundred meters off the dirt track. Katrina Leatham, one of the Bubye River ranch managers, was driving that day. Her husband, Blondie, was in the passenger seat. Katrina and

Blondie had built a nursery for orphaned rhino calves at Mazunga. That's where I met and bottle-fed "Lisa" and "Carla," the two young females we had translocated on an earlier mission.

Feeding hand-reared black rhino orphans at Bubye River Conservancy.

In addition to my lesson in rhino acoustics, I was struck by all the warthogs that lived in their operation. Snuffle, snuffle, snort, snort. If you were caught unaware, you'd end up with a snout between your legs and, like as not, you'd go down like tenpins.

On this fateful day, Katrina and Blondie joined their daughter, Lauren, Kobus, me, Chap, John, Natasha, and Norman English, the Bubye River conservator. To say there were too many of us was an understatement. The ear notching, blood drawing, measuring, and everything else went quickly and smoothly.

Working on a black rhino baby. Vet Chap Masterson on left, vet Kobus on right, and vet Lauren in back with a thermometer up its bum, 2013.

We were all pretty tired at the end of a long day. Chap prepared to reverse the M99, so we all strolled back to the vehicle to keep our requisite distance. I climbed up into the high bench seats behind the cab and rested my hand on the roll bar. Katrina got behind the wheel. Blondie got into the passenger seat. Norman climbed in the back, just in front of the tailgate. Lauren and Kobus stood on the ground behind the tailgate waiting for Chap to administer the reversal drug.

Chap reversed the baby rhino and ran back to stand with Lauren and Kobus. Not a good decision, as it turned out. I watched the baby through my Zeiss binocs, which have really good lenses. She popped up onto her feet like a bloody jack-in-the-box springing from its box. She charged left and stopped. Then she turned and charged right until she was right behind the mopane tree next to where she had snoozed. Through my binoculars I saw her head turn. Her left eye was staring straight at me.

I started to pound the cab and yell, "She's coming. Get the truck moving! Let's go! Let's go!"

That sixteen-month-old, 800-pound rhino launched out from behind that mopane like a thoroughbred leaping out of the starting gate. I watched her instantly take off into a gallop, her front legs churning the ground. Within seconds she must have reached over thirty miles an hour.

Katrina started the truck and slammed it in gear. The three vets managed to jump in the vehicle just in time. We took off around acacias with the rhino closing in and slaloming in sync with our steering.

Suddenly Katrina slowed the truck. A log blocked our path. The rhino was on us instantly and slammed the tailgate with a mighty crash. Katrina turned the wheel and the vehicle was flying again, the rhino running alongside us, huffing and puffing like *The Little Engine That Could*. She veered off a few seconds later and slowed to a stop.

We continued onto the road and pulled up.

Norman was picking acacia thorns out of his left hand—we must have swiped a bush. We all looked at each other with that kind of "did that really just happen?" look. And then we all started shouting at once.

Lauren was shouting, "It was in the cab with us! Did I really see that?"

Norman responded with the same incredulousness. "Her head and right front leg were over the tailgate! I placed my right hand on her head and pushed her back out as she popped up in the air."

I had missed the opportunity of a lifetime! If only I had hit "movie" on my camera instead of mashing the button while it was in picture mode, I could have caught the chaos on film! I'd be a YouTube sensation. Instead, I came away with one motion-blurred frame of god-knows-what.

We climbed down and looked at the tailgate. There, dented and scratched into the paint job, was the X-shaped gouge from her horn. About six inches to the right was another X. She had contacted the tailgate twice.

What impressed me most was that the baby rhino had instinctively stopped short of simply bulldozing the truck. On impact she had twisted her head in the X motion that rhinos use to eviscerate their victims. And she did it twice—so fast that none of us remembers the second impact. Hot damn!

Norman English, Bubye River Conservator (bloody hand) pointing at the X impact of rhino baby that hit the tailgate and pitched halfway into the rear, 2013.

That was a close call. What happened two days later was worse by far. On the last day of Rhino Ops 2013, I came within about three seconds of being run down by a 3,000-pound black rhino cow who was defending her calf.

It started off as a pretty typical baby operation. We had two extra volunteers with us, Sam, an intern for Norman English, and his girlfriend visiting from Britain. They accompanied Tasha and me. About an hour after our less-than-delicious lunch (boiled eggs and nasty heavily buttered, processed meat sandwiches), the radio came alive. Charlie Two had found a cow and calf. The calf looked to be the right age and location to be the last of the year's baby crop to be cataloged.

Sierra Oscar took off, circled around, and showed Tasha the direction to the rhino. Radios were not working very well that day.

We all mobilized: *Vroom, vroom. Whirr, whirr.* The helicopter and the Husky flew northwest. We headed west in the Land Cruiser, looking for the best cross-track, likely an old fence-line road from cattle days, to head north. Raoul circled back periodically, talking to Tasha, trying to find a way for us to access the site. It took about forty minutes.

Finally, we were all in place. John took the helicopter in and Chap darted the calf. John turned Romeo Lima Zulu and ran the cow off, as Tasha drove us to within running distance of the male calf. He nobly ran this way and that to avoid us—mostly in circles—finally plopped down about eight minutes after being darted just short of a little mopane tree. I looked around. The countryside was covered with immature mopane— not a tree in sight big enough to climb.

The four of us ran in with our gear and got to work on the rhino. I was in charge of the jet sprayer and counting respirations (of course!), Sam managed the thermometer, and Tasha started measurements. Out of the corner of my eye I saw John walk up with the rest of the vet supplies. He had just about reached the head of the rhino when he looked over the shrubs, spun around, and ran like the devil was chasing him!

Not the devil, just the 3,000-pound cow bursting through a thorn bush, heading full bore and straight toward the ass end of her calf. Right where I was pumping the sprayer. I figure she was running at thirty miles per hour and the bush was about one hundred feet from me. That's about two or three seconds of life remaining before I would be squashed like a bug.

Tasha screamed at the top of her lungs. Sam and girlfriend scattered to the left. I dropped the sprayer, spun, and ran like hell in the opposite direction. I was totally panicked! There was not a single tree big enough to climb. My back was turned to her and she could be on me in two heartbeats. I slid to my knees behind a little mopane, maybe twelve feet tall and turned around to face the rhino, hoping she would run past me and not right over the little tree.

Our scattering like quail must have confused her. As I looked up, she was sliding to a stop in a cloud of dust. Her distance from Tasha was only fifteen feet. She was about twice that from me, and about twenty-five feet from the kids. We were all holding our collective breath. Suddenly we heard the helicopter start up. The rhino cow flung her magnificent head from side to side, extremely agitated. Then turned around and trotted off.

How's that for a close call? All in a day's work, I say.

We dusted ourselves off and went back to the task at hand—processing that little boy rhino, number twenty-two, and the last one of the season. I think Sam had a couple of acacia thorns stuck in his forearm, but other than that, we were uninjured. Hell, I wasn't even all that dirty!

That evening, drinking the last of our scotch, Chap paid me a huge compliment.

"Ed, last year I was not impressed by you. You were slow and didn't seem to be up to the work. Afterward, I found out that you had caught the flu from Tasha and had been running a fever for those three days. Sick as a dog, you never complained, working 'til you were ready to drop."

He paused and looked at me kindly.

"This year you had two of the closest calls we've ever experienced—and you seemed to love it!"

"Well, Chap," I replied, my heart swelling, "you know how I define a great adventure, don't you?"

Chap looked at me wryly. "And what is that?"

I started laughing before I could spit it out. "I survived! Oh my God, I survived!"

—

The season was over. Early the next morning, I said good-bye to my friends and flew back to Harare with Raoul. By noon I was at Harare International, shaking Raoul's hand, and on my way back to the States.

When I got home, a little more than a day later, one of the first things I said to Jackie was, "You know, I think this is the last time for me. I don't think I'll return next year."

Jackie looked up from the watercolor she was working on and gave me a knowing look. "Yeah, right," she said.

Epilogue

IT'S BEEN MORE THAN A year since I started writing down these stories. 2014 was a wonderful year for me. I helped Jackie celebrate a big birthday while we traveled through Ireland. I went to Indonesia twice, the second time as a volunteer on an eighteen-day research cruise during which we collected data on fish, coral reefs, and turtle beaches within a new marine protected area. You might ask, "why coral reef research?" My standard answer is always "Because I can." The only thing I didn't do in 2014 was Rhino Ops.

Just as Jackie had predicted, I couldn't stay away. I left my entire month of July unbooked so I could return for another season. Unfortunately, a combination of permitting problems and logistics delayed Rhino Ops until the middle of August, right when I had planned an Indonesian scuba adventure.

As you may know, rhino conservation suffered a bad year of poaching in 2014. Namibian rhinos were hit by poachers for the first time. South Africa lost more than twelve hundred, mostly white, rhinos. Kruger National Park resembled a war zone. Poachers in South Africa have become more sophisticated, using veterinarians, sedatives, and helicopters in their efforts to steal horn. The occurrence of gunfights between rangers (and army) and poachers has been on the rise. Poaching has returned to Bubye River Conservancy and has increased in Save Valley Conservancy. In Zimbabwe, the rule of law has continued to suffer under the gangster government of Robert Mugabe.

It is difficult to be optimistic about the future. But there is some hope. The rhino population in Zimbabwe has continued to increase under Raoul du Toit and Natasha Anderson's constant vigilance and total dedication. Zim is now home to the fourth largest population of black rhinos on earth.

I pledge to contribute the net proceeds of *Running with Rhinos* to the Lowveld Rhino Trust, through the wonderful oversight of Dr. Susie Ellis and her staff at the International Rhino Foundation, and to other conservation efforts.

If you would like to make a contribution, please contact:

Dr. Susie Ellis, Ex. Dir.
The International Rhino Foundation
201 Main Street, Suite 2600
Fort Worth TX 76102
www.rhinos.org

Donations to be directed to:

The Lowveld Rhino Trust
c/o The Sand County Foundation
131 W. Wilson St, Suite 610
Madison, WI 53703
www.sandcounty.net

Author Q & A

1. How and when did you first know you wanted to write *Running with Rhinos*? Can you speak a bit about that, and about your aspirations for the book?

   I was preparing to write a book review for "The Bloomsbury Review" on what I saw as an author's superficial experience with rhinos. It motivated me to tell a more detailed story of working with rhinos in the African bush. I hope readers see Running with Rhinos *as honest storytelling.*

2. Would you describe one or two people who will always hold a special place for you when you remember your adventures with the rhinos, and why they are special to you?

   Without a doubt, Raoul and Natasha. I love to work with passionate, competent people.

3. Can you speak to how the thrills, dangers, and achievements you've experienced with the rhinos have changed you and your view of the world?

   Actually, the tragedies and failures I've experienced in my life have had the most profound effect, not my achievements. I think it is dangerous to make too much of achievements: You might mistakenly believe you know what you're doing.

4. Could you expand on your statement that "Walking on the savanna touches a primal connection to one million years of evolution. For me, it is a coming home."

We are descended from Hominids who evolved over the last several million years on the savannas of Africa. Our immediate ancestor, Homo erectus, is the first true human, capable of using tools, controlling fire, developing culture. Homo erectus spread out from Africa across the old world. Modern man, Homo sapiens—who followed them out of Africa 900,000 years later—may have driven them to extinction. When I sit around a campfire in the bush, I feel that deep connection. I don't feel nearly as connected driving on the highway.

5. You stated, "I want to climb Lingai, the soda carbonate volcano near Natron. My bucket list keeps growing!" Would you comment on how it feels to have had so many experiences that would definitely be on many people's bucket lists, and whether you think you will ever stop adding things to your list?

A shrink once asked me, "Ed, when is enough?" I replied to her, "I suppose when I'm dead."

6. What do you hope is the most important message readers will take away after finishing your book?

Conservation without sustainable livelihoods for the people living with iconic wild creatures will not succeed. A rhino must be seen as more valuable alive than dead.

7. What would be your advice to people of all ages who wish to make a positive impact on endangered animals?

Westerners have a lot to learn from African people and the wildlife with which they live. Also, I recommend every student take a year or two off and work, intern, or volunteer in the third world. They might realize that the luckiest break in their entire lives was their choice of parents. I hope that the discovery of this incredible advantage will bring the humility necessary to accomplish great things.

8. Could you describe the qualities of the people you worked alongside in Africa and why those qualities make them different from those who have jobs in more ordinary settings?

   The first thing I noticed was that Africans are both entrepreneurial and optimistic. Considering the difficulties of their lives, that realization blew my hair back.

9. What do you think gangster governments mean for the future of conservation and for Africa in general? What do you hope for the future of conservation efforts?

   We cannot save Africa from bad governments. Africans must evolve forms of government that work for them. Until they do, the wildlife will remain at risk.

10. Have you ever considered living in Africa permanently? Why or why not?

    My wife and I planned to build a house on the Save Valley Conservancy. We built stone ramps to the top of a low granite kopje only to be halted by the gangster government of Zimbabwe. Our ramps provided a perfect path for the local elephants to access and eat all the trees that grew around the crest. I'm glad they got something out of our failed endeavor!

11. It was shocking and slightly terrifying to read your description of the veterinary sedative M99, and how a single drop of it on human skin could be fatal. Can you describe what it was like for you to cope with the knowledge of its potency while being present when the drug was being used in the rescues?

    I've been accused of being born without a fear gene. I do try to arm myself with as much knowledge as I can before I do something really dangerous. Thus, I'll work around the drugs but not administer them.

12. The education you shared in the book in terms of being exposed to so much fascinating geology and flora was impressive. Can you talk a bit about what it was like to learn so much in a hands-on setting?

   From the time I was ten years old, I've loved learning about nature firsthand. Nature led me to books and formal education, not the other way around.

13. Did you have a favorite chapter to write in *Running with Rhinos*? If so, could you comment on why it was your favorite?

   I suppose, "Romeo Hotel." I really admire Antonia. Maybe writing that story was a form of therapy as her visit was somewhat traumatic for all the men involved, including me.

14. Do you have another book waiting in the wings? If so, can you tell us a bit about it?

   I've been writing for about thirty-five years. It probably comes from being taught storytelling at a summer camp when I was fourteen years old. My children sat around many campfires in the high country of Colorado listening to my tales. It was a natural progression to begin writing them down. My career in geology and backcountry fieldwork led me to many adventures. If this book is successful, I hope my readers will want to hear more about the less traveled trails I've walked.

15. With "smuggler" and "gunrunner" on your CV, how does it feel to now have "author" among your job titles?

   When I started writing Running with Rhinos *I didn't expect it to affect me. But it has. It seems to have closed a loop from thinking to doing to writing and now to publishing.*